ME, MY BOYS AND GOD

DWIGHT R MOSS

BALBOA.PRESS
A DIVISION OF HAY HOUSE

Balboa Press books may be ordered through booksellers or by contacting:

Balboa Press
A Division of Hay House
1663 Liberty Drive
Bloomington, IN 47403
www.balboapress.com
844-682-1282

Unless otherwise noted, all scriptural references contained in this book are drawn from the New International Version (NIV) and full credit is given to that edition.

Print information available on the last page.

ISBN: 979-8-7652-4069-4 (sc)
ISBN: 979-8-7652-4068-7 (e)

Balboa Press rev. date: 05/03/2023

ACKNOWLEDGEMENT

I am very thankful to Candace Hardin Littlejohn who made many contributions and edited this material over the last year.

I am also very thankful to Marilyn McCord who reviewed and edited this book in its early stages.

Additionally, my wife, Maureen, has been my right arm in getting <u>Me, My Boys and God</u> to completion. I am very thankful for her diligence and perseverance in seeing the book to completion. Maureen is a beautiful and gracious partner.

Finally, I am most thankful to my beautiful daughter, Julia, for bringing these boys into my life.

CONTENTS

FOREWORD

I love my children and my grandchildren dearly. I believe that they will try to comfort me when the door is closing on this temporary life that I am living. One day their door on this life will begin to close. How I wish I could comfort them in that hour. Humanly speaking, that will be impossible.

God does not deal with impossible. With him all things are possible. The door on this life is closing. How fast it will close I do not know. I do know this; however, I am the brother of the eternal Jesus. The eternal God is my Father! We have become inseparable. Now I know that not a hair of my head will be harmed when my door closes. My friends, my journey is eternal. God has bestowed upon me the power of his life. I am an eternal child of God.

When the door of this life begins to close on my children or grandchildren, my prayer for them is that they will have entered into an intimate and passionate love affair with Jesus and the Father. I pray for the peace and love of God to overshadow their lives forever.

I can only truly relate to my own reality. What I have discovered is that there is a life that can take me and mine beyond our personal experiences.

I have not experienced life after death. So, how can I speak of such things? Religion cannot take me into that experience. My own human effort cannot carry me there. If I said I know a man that can take me beyond my experiences in life, the world would deny it. If I said that I know a man who was victorious over death, the world would doubt it. Then, I would say to the world read Matthew, Mark, Luke and John and prove them wrong.

Most people come to a place where they ultimately want truth. You may not even be aware of it. However, deep within your heart and soul you are yearning for truth. Most likely when you receive a truth, you do not immediately realize that you have encountered it. You may have just realized that your old way of thinking was biased and prejudiced because of your personal experiences in life.

When I began, _Me, My Boys and God_, I had no idea where the writing would lead me. I had been studying and submitting articles for the <u>Clay County Progress</u> from the book of John chapter 13. I paused and began to reflect on how God teaches.

If you believe in scripture, you know that we are in the time period told by Jeremiah 31:31-34. We live in a time when God is the teacher. His lessons may come through men and women in the flesh. However, if the teaching is true to the heart of God, it comes from God, through the conduit of the Holy Spirit of Truth.

What I have written concerning the way God teaches is not of my own understanding. I cannot write of eternal things unless I have help from the one who was in the beginning with God. The apostle John says that Jesus is God. I call him my brother, of perfect, sinless flesh, who reveals God's truth.

There are some personal things in this writing that reflects on how I see God as my teacher. God has taught me through many people, but he came to me through infants and little children. You might ask; "How can this be?" Well, Nicodemus, a very educated Pharisee, asked Jesus the same question in John 3:9. Jesus was sharing with Nicodemus the necessity of being born again, born new or born of God.

The necessity of a new birth is because our experiences in life are limited to human experiences. Before we can begin to experience spiritual things, we must be born of God. Matthew, Mark, Luke and John had come into the inner realm of God. In order to fully grasp their words, you must first be born again of God. Jesus told Nicodemus that he could not see the Kingdom of God unless he was first born of God. Nicodemus needed not a fleshly rebirth, but to be born as a new person in the image and teachings of God before salvation could be revealed to him.

I am now experiencing eternal revelations from God. As a man, it is amazing to me how God can teach one through a child. I imagine from God's perspective; it is just everyday work. God knows that when the student is ready to receive, the teacher will appear. Are you ready to be taught by God? If so, the teacher has appeared. It is not me. This teacher is the Holy Spirit of Truth sent from the Father and the Son. Are you ready for your lessons?

Open your heart and your mind to new possibilities. Realities! Let God teach you with his love, his kindness, his knowledge and wisdom.

More than anything in life I want my boys, my family and my friends to know the one true God and to be known by God. I did not get to this place overnight. I have been walking, running and talking with Jesus. He is my brother. He lives with me, and he lives in me. He has shown me beautiful places I cannot fathom how to get there alone. However, this Spirit of God will show me the way into the paradise of God. There is an unexplainable joy in knowing that you are safe and secure in the hands of God.

I love my wife and all my family. I love all my boys and all my girls. However, God saw fit to teach me many things through a growing ten-month-old child. When God uses a small child to teach you about his love, you have been educated. I was Sean's provider of all things for a period of time. I had always loved him, but then that love grew. Sean and I became close because of the circumstances and experiences of life. We were a twosome for a while. God knew what he was doing.

Sean could not do very much or give very much. He was small, innocent, helpless as babies are. As I cared for him and loved him, he loved me back. One of my wife's sayings comes to mind: "I cannot give what I have not received". Well! Sean was receiving love and he was giving back with full measure. When he returned my love, I loved him all the more. He became the apple of my eye and melted my heart.

One day I was looking at Sean. My heart was pouring out into the atmosphere a deep, passionate, enduring love. Then my eyes were opened. I knew without a doubt that I was the apple of my Father's eye. I knew that through this child God was teaching me how much he loved me.

My God's love is passionate and enduring. He is pouring out his heart into me. He wants me to love him back the way that I love this child. Actually, God wants me to love him more so that He can give me more of his pure and perfect love, so I can give, and Sean can receive the pure, perfect love of God into his heart.

I want you, the reader, to know this. Nothing can separate you from the love of God that is in Christ Jesus. It reaches beyond death because death has no power over the love of God, and it cannot claim the life that exists in God's love. I invite you to journey with me, my boys and God. May the eternal Spirit reveal to you, places in your heart and mind, where you have never gone before.

ONE

IT IS GOOD FOR MAN TO BE ALONE

W hen God teaches us, it comes from many unexpected avenues. He taught me that I did not know Him. I denied that He existed while serving in Vietnam. Death was as common as eating dinner. It was years later that God intervened in my life and revealed himself to me. It was not in church or at any religious activity that he came to me. I was on a long run, trying to make sense of life's challenges. God broke through my fortified wall which I had built to resist all religious advances, and I became quite successful in this resistance.

However, my cocoon from religion had no defenses that could repel the God of love. He broke through to lead me to Jesus, the Man of Truth. God used little children and an infant to bring me closer to the heart of his deep, paternal love. He taught me about relationships through the eyes of children.

Thirty-eight months ago, I found myself alone with three boys. Their ages were 10 months, 3 years and 5 months, and 5 years and three months. I was a Pastor of a small ministry. Coming from a family where I was the oldest of eight children probably laid some of the foundation for being able to deal with young children.

When my daughter came to my home, she was accompanied by the two boys, Jacques and Jaden. It would be about two and a half years before Sean was born.

At the time I was living alone. I was working on some pre-class assignments for a theology course at Emory. It was this course that prompted the letter to God. Anyway, I was sitting in my glider chair. It was winter. I was in front of a wood heater with a glass door. The flames were dancing. I was toasty, comfortable and lonely.

My prayer began with an apology to God. You might ask. Don't you mean repent? I do not mean that I was repenting. I was apologizing. We often say that there is no presence greater than the presence of God. With all my heart, I sincerely believe that is true. However, even God said that it is not good for man to be alone. I believe that this is equally true for a woman.

I apologized to God because even in his presence I needed a human touch. We are made to desire companionship. This is one of the beautiful gifts of God. Without the inner connection of people and the desire for that connection, we would become emotionally cold and self- centered.

If you believe in scripture, you believe that when two people are married, they become one in union with God. This does not mean that there are not two separate identities. Jesus and the Father are one, yet they are separate. What makes them one is their unity of purpose. This is a key to marriage. For a marriage to be truly successful there must exist unity of purpose.

For the Christian marriage to be truly successful, each partner should be willing to seek the will and purpose of God for their life. In the flesh, we see this as giving up our own will and purpose. From the devil's marketing strategy this is what he wants you to believe. However, humans are made in the likeness of God.

In the fall, Adam and Eve chose to follow the flesh and Satan. Let us not be too quick to judge them as we are in the New Covenant Era. Jesus has corrected the wrong. The curse that Adam and Eve brought upon us has been conquered and destroyed.

However, Satan is thrilled by the cunning that he used to deceive Adam and Eve and he continues to use it. Although we are created in the image of God, Satan told Adam and Eve that if they ate the fruit, they would become like God. In Genesis 1:26, 27, we see that we were created in God's image. We were already likened to God. So, the great lie continues.

As humans who are created in God's image, we are incomplete vessels until we come into alignment with God. To follow the will and purpose of God is not a demand of God. It is an invitation to become a partner with God.

This is what I find so amazing. He does not demand anything from you. What God wants to do is give something to you. All of this will, and purpose of God is useless until you receive his gift.

The gift that God offers is undoing of the penalty of death, fear, darkness, anxiety and lies. Until you receive his gift, you cannot do his will and fulfill his purpose. Neither can you know to seek it

THE GIFT THAT GOD WANTS TO GIVE YOU IS HIMSELF.

In John chapter 13 God in the person of Jesus Christ is bowed down before humanity. This God, this Jesus demonstrates for us as he approaches the climax of his physical life that God loves you with all of his heart, all of his mind, and all of his strength. When Jesus on the cross said, *"It is finished"* (Jn. 19:30b). He had given us his mind, his body and his spirit. He gave all of himself (Jn. 3:16). Jesus makes it plain that the flesh counts for nothing, when compared to the gift of the eternal life and the Holy Spirit of God. It is this Spirit that is a transforming Spirit. It is the Holy Spirit that begins to develop your mind and begins to bring you into alignment with God. This is not a demanding Spirit. This is not a controlling Spirit. This is a Spirit that will help you to see that your greater purpose will not be achieved by human effort. It can only be achieved by the Holy Spirit of God that you allow to guide your life.

TWO

HEART ADJUSTMENT

My prayer that evening as I sat alone was more of a conversation than a prayer. I confess that I just did not like living alone. My conversation was about more than just having company. My message to God was pretty direct. I did not just want company: I wanted a particular kind of company.

I had been talking with God about how much I needed a companion. I got pretty explicit. He had to know that I missed the touch of a woman. He had to know that I was lonely and that I needed to fill a void in my life. I could almost smell the fragrance of a woman. I knew that I really needed a woman in my life. However, do Christians not believe that God knows our needs better than we do? I do believe that he can see right in through the portal of our hearts. When he looks, he knows best how to fill a void for those who truly love him and seek his ways.

In between my heart to heart with God, Reico, a past boyfriend of my daughter, called. He was a charming young black man with a very nice smile, but he was more than just a boyfriend. He was the father of her two beautiful young boys. To be truthful, he had two older children. However, these two boys were my daughter's boys too. And so that makes me their grandfather. Not too complicated. It is just life in this twenty-first century.

What about the call? Reico called to give me a heads up that my daughter was headed my way with the boys, Jacques and Jaden!

I hung up and continued talking with God about how much I needed a companion. I got pretty explicit.

As Christians, do we not believe that our Father in heaven will teach us all truth through the Spirit of Truth? Jesus said that the Father would send us an advocate for truth that would teach us everything (see Jn. 14:26). For me, at the time, my truth was that I needed a woman in my life. Maybe God was waiting for the adjustment of my heart to bring my mind into alignment with the true desire of my inner heart. Just maybe, my Father wanted to adjust my thinking to the point that I would pray for the woman. Not just a woman, but the woman that my Father chooses. Do I believe that my Father knows best?

At the end of the day, my daughter is on the way with two boys. I had no idea what God was going to teach me as He began to turn my life upside down. I have heard it said that God's ways are higher than our ways. Some say that God's thinking is upside down compared to human thought. I believe that it is upside down, sideways and backwards when compared to human ways and thoughts.

When I think about it, there is no way to compare God's ways with human ways. They are not biologically different. God is not biological. So, humanly speaking, there is no way to compare God's ways with our ways. Our Father is in a completely different dimension. How can we compare the temporary human existence with the timeless existence of God? We cannot. That would be like comparing light to darkness or comparing life to death. Eternity has nothing in common with time. That is, eternal existence has no commonality with a time bound existence. How can light be dark? How can life be death?

In history there is only one man who entered into a time bound period of existence, while at the same time, He knew that his true identity was revealed in a life that was not bound or controlled by time. He came to reveal to me that my true existence was not in the prison of time. He reveals to the human life that our true existence is a dimension of timelessness. What my Father was going to teach me about was his dimension that is before and beyond time? It is impossible for the human mind to grasp the ways of God. That is what led the apostle Paul to say, *"Who can know the mind of God?"* He went on to say that we have the mind of Christ available to us. It is this mind that knows the limited human dimension as well as the dimension that is not bound by time.

In between the call from Reico and my daughter's arrival, I was interrupted again. I heard a knock at my door. The weather was cold. Snow was on the ground. I was met by a man who was warmly dressed. He was of medium build, needed a shave and had a couple of teeth missing. He said that he had been put out of his house and he was homeless. He wanted to know if I knew of any place that he could stay. I do not remember our conversation except that when he was leaving, I did tell him that if he didn't find anything by the end of the day, come back here. There was another person in a vehicle who was giving him a ride. I closed the door. In my mind, I figured that if someone was giving him a ride, they would surely be able to help him find a place to stay.

THE ARRIVAL

When my daughter arrived, I became very much aware that I was in the human dimension. The house was no longer quiet. She arrived in the early afternoon. We got busy getting everyone settled in upstairs. Time was flying by.

We made it through the afternoon. Dinner was over. Clean-up was done. It was time for showers and some quiet time before bed. The boys seemed ok despite having suffered through fiery debates between the parents. I can see Jacques' smile. Jaden is quieter. However, his heart was hungry for positive attention. He would not make the first move, but I can see his eyes light up and a smile cross that little boy's face when he gets a warm hug.

Well, Father, this is not exactly what I had in mind, but you have dispelled the loneliness and there is certainly a new kind of warmth in the house. Even now hearts are being molded. From the boys' standpoint, there is no doubt that they felt welcome and safe. I believe that this became their first real home as our hearts begin to beat as a family. The day was not over. As I look back, I certainly believe that surely God has a sense of humor.

ANOTHER KNOCK AT THE DOOR

I was startled to hear another knock at the door. It was dark. My daughter and the boys were wrapping up the evening. I walked slowly to the door, flipped on the light and there in my carport he stood, the man from earlier in the afternoon.

He was standing in my carport at the door. His driver had turned the truck around and was headed back down the driveway. The man had with him a travel bag. The man who I had told to come back if he did not find a place to stay. I have thought about this and as I got to know the man, I sincerely believe that he and his driver friend spent the day keeping warm and waiting for night fall, hoping that surely, I was a man of my word.

WHO IN THE WORLD!

Be careful what you pray for! I think God did not hear my complete prayer. What would unfold was nothing like what I originally had in mind. Maybe my mind was just a little lustful and just maybe it needed to be adjusted. When I said that I was lonely, I was thinking of a woman. However, as I look back, my Father was thinking of a heart adjustment.

Had I not also prayed Father help me to know Jesus more intimately? Immediately after praying to know Jesus more deeply and realizing what I had prayed, I said "Father have mercy on me." I had prayed this prayer one day while washing and drying dishes. I had a dish in my hand. I was drying it. As I turned toward the cabinet to put the dish away, I realized what I had prayed.

When I prayed to know Jesus more intimately, I knew that to know him was to suffer with him, to die with him. It had to be a death of willing submission, to crucify my old life so that I could rise with him into the new life of Christ. My Father knew what I needed. He knew that in the depth of my heart, I needed more of my Father's love. He also knew that to receive this love, understand this love, and live this love I would have to go with Jesus all the way.

My daughter and the boys had moved into a large bonus room with limited closet space, but it had a balcony. Fortunately, I had another guest room. I invited my newfound friend to a place in the vacant bedroom. I wonder if God was laughing. A real Christian should love and pray for their enemies and open their hearts to strangers. To be honest, I am not sure that my heart was in line with my actions as I showed the stranger to the room that would no longer be empty.

That night as I laid down in my bed, I began to speak to God. My mind was in a whirlwind. I certainly was not lonely. Within twenty-four hours, God had answered my prayer about being lonely. In one day, my home had gone from one person to five. My aloneness, humanly speaking, had improved four hundred percent. It has been said that when a student is ready to be taught, the teacher will appear.

I know and I believe that we are in the era of God's new covenant. This means that those who receive Christ into their lives will now be taught by God. The prophet Jeremiah spoke about this in Jeremiah 31:31-34. When Jesus descended to the earth, we begin to see the implementation of this new era. When He came, God began to teach us in a way that was two dimensional. Jesus in spirit is not bound by time. Jesus became a time-bound man in the flesh. However, Jesus spoke the language of God. Even his own body did not see decay. However, according to scripture it had to go through a transition.

When Jesus had taken his body up from its death, it was the spiritual Jesus who in the Father's will took his body up again. When Jesus revealed himself to Mary, Jesus told her not to hold on to him because he had not ascended to the Father (Jn. 20:17). Later, Jesus invited Thomas to touch him. The body of Jesus had undergone a transition. I do not know or understand what happened. However, I do believe that one day I too will ascend to the Father and receive a transformed body. Jesus has already told me that which is verifiably true. My flesh counts for nothing. However, his Spirit of truth that is in me brings me into the place of eternal existence. The word Christian means, "Christ-Like."

The next day I did not fully realize that my life was in a new era. I had no idea about the bumps and curves of life, or of the hills I would climb. There would be mountains and there would be valleys. We settled in together: my daughter, my grandsons, and a stranger. This stranger was supposed to be looking for work and a place to live. However, he seemed very content. He was not motivated to find a job or a place to live. After all, life was pretty good for him. Why mess it up?

THREE

WORRY! DEPRESSING WASTE OF TIME

One morning I had been up for some time. My daughter was enrolled at Tri County Community college. She was up and out. The boys were enrolled at Elf Day Care. I was either doing something related to real estate or writing and studying. I heard a noise. I looked up at the stairs and our guest was coming down in his house robe. No need to get dressed! It is only midmorning. This man was probably in his mid to late forties. In my mind it is reasonable to expect that a man this age would be seeking a way to be productive and support himself. Maybe he was taking Jesus' words of saying do not worry about tomorrow a little too casually! After all he had a roof, a comfortable bed, hot showers and food. Why should he be concerned?

Well, Jesus went on to say there is trouble enough for each day (see Mat. 6:34). The problem here was not tomorrow. The problem was today for my stranger friend! We really did become friends. However, I'll just call the stranger who was no longer a stranger, "friend." My friend was homeless, but not at the moment! He had no food of his own, but not at the moment! Why worry? When you have a roof, a bed, a hot shower and food, God is good. I looked at Mathew 6:34 where Jesus said that each day has enough trouble of its own. As my friend descended the stairs, I realized that he was not approaching the day as if he had a problem or problems to be solved. God is good. It is cold outside, but I am not outside, and there is plenty of food and drinks. The people here are friendly and accommodating. God has been good to them and so they are being good to me. Today life is good for him!

He did not have a clue about my troubles of the day. The reason that I was not worrying about tomorrow was because I was facing the challenges of this day. I know that when I turn on the light, I have to pay the cost. Mortgage interest ticks on each day. Utility bills accumulate. The car payment is getting closer every day. Taxes are accumulating each day. Every day there is less food remaining. It will need to be restocked. How can I not worry about tomorrow?

I do not worry about tomorrow because as I face the problems of the day, I know tomorrow will be ok, because today I am working on the problems of tomorrow. When tomorrow comes, I will face those problems then. Why should I worry about tomorrow? Since my friend cannot see the problems of today, he will awake one day in a tomorrow which has become today, and he will wonder what happened to the roof, the warmth, the hot showers and the food. Then, the tomorrow that becomes today will be "enough trouble of its own".

Again, I look and see a man with a smile coming down the stairs. My daughter and the boys are long gone. My friend is still in his robe. For a person who has always felt a need to be productive, I am beginning to become very uncomfortable with the picture that I see.

Why would I be uncomfortable? I am made in the likeness of God. I wonder if God gets uncomfortable with me? Jesus also gave us the example of using what God has given you in a profitable way. We only need to look at Mathew 25:14-30 to help us understand that instead of worrying about tomorrow, we should concern ourselves with what we should do today.

In the parable of the Bags of Gold in the gospel of Matthew 24:14-30, a man presumed to be wealthy has decided to go on a journey. In this story the man entrusted his wealth to three servants. The NIV describes it as five bags of gold to one person, two bags of gold to a second person, and one bag to a third person. The story indicates that the master gave each one according to his ability.

When the master returned and it became time to settle his accounts with the servants, two had done well, investing what was entrusted to them. The third person had done nothing with his bag of gold except to hide it in the ground. The third man was not facing the trouble of the present day. His master gave him according to his ability. He had the ability to manage the one bag of gold. When the man told the master that he had buried the gold for safe keeping, the master called him a wicked, lazy servant as he had not produced anything with what had been entrusted to him.

Each servant had a decision to make. Each had to decide how he would handle what the master had entrusted in his care. Each needed to make a decision for the present day. He could not perform tomorrow today. You cannot begin in any tomorrow of the future. The time you begin will always be the present time of today. You cannot quit smoking tomorrow or next month. The day you quit will be today.

Most lives are spent in thoughts about tomorrow. We think about our future. We plan. We say that we are going to do great things. However, our sights are on our tomorrows. The trouble is pushing past today and getting started.

When my daughter (now thirty-six years old) was about fourteen years old, I was recovering from a serious ankle injury that I had received bounding down an embankment. My daughter asked me about doing a local 5-K race. I always perked up when she wanted to do something positive. I was not sure if I could do it. I had been walking my driveway with difficulty. As the 5-k approached, I decided that I would try to do a three-and-a-half-mile loop from my driveway.

I began walking. As I loosened up, I would do some pick up shuffles (no real speed). I kept moving at what my ankle would allow. As I moved, I made up my own personal proverb. It goes like this, "You can't do what you can't do, however, you can do what you can do. So, if you do what you can do today, what you can't do today, maybe you can do tomorrow." From a physical standpoint, I invested today's ability. I could only do what I could do. Tomorrow came and my daughter and I did a 5-K run. By using today's ability, your tomorrows will be blessed by what you invest in this day.

Was God smiling? He knew that my compassion was being used up. Was I really the master of my household? Did I expect each person who resided there to do something productive each day? My guest did not seem to be worried about tomorrow. Nor did he seem to have any problems to solve for today.

When Jesus said do not worry about tomorrow, to me he was saying that worrying is a depressing waste of time. The fact is worry accomplishes nothing. However, probably all of us have at some time been affected by worry. What is the best antidote to worry? For me it is to do something productive. It could be a workout, sorting junk mail, bills or posting the bills for payment. It could be just getting started on a project. Just do something with the most important gift that God has given you. That is your body, mind and spirit.

In the parable of the bags of gold (or talents), it was the producers that were blessed. They did not worry about the master's return. Their master challenged them with opportunities based on their ability. Two accepted the challenge and went to work, the other one was worried about his master's return on some tomorrow. So, on each today he did nothing. One could say that Mathew 7:25-34 and Mathew 24:14-30 are in conflict. They are not. Just because Jesus says that you should not worry about tomorrow does not mean that you should not invest the gifts that you have been given today.

The parable in Mathew 25:14 - 30 ends with the lazy servant's gold being given to the person with ten bags, Jesus makes a statement that we may wonder about "*to those who have will more be given, and those who have not what they have will be taken from them*". This may not seem fair. However, it is a natural rule of our human existence. A runner does not just go out and compete until he has developed his body to a higher level. He must train, eat right, and get proper rest. In the end he will have more of a body to compete with. On the other hand, someone who does nothing with their body will begin to lose the strength and energy that they have.

It became apparent that my guest was content with his new life. He was not worried about tomorrow. On the other hand, he was not living a productive life.

My guest kept telling me that he was not having any luck when I asked him about finding a place. I am a pretty easy-going person, and I am compassionate.

Satan can use the beautiful gift of compassion that comes from God to mess with you. At one time, he used my gift of compassion to judge myself more compassionate than God. This led to denial that there was a God. Satan even used the idea of being like God to trip up Adam and Eve when, in fact, they were created in God's image.

I balanced my checking account, had a workout and had eaten breakfast. I was studying and writing. I heard movement. I looked at the stairs. My guest was coming down in his bath robe. He had a smile and a warm good morning. I knew that I had been procrastinating. Something had to change!

I think my Father in heaven decided to help me out. My guest at some point began drinking my beer. I noticed this quickly because a sixpack will last me a week or two. I confronted him. He said that he would stop. It wasn't long when I was entering the house at the carport door which led me by the stairs to the basement that I encountered my guest coming up the stairs with a beer in his hand. We had a serious discussion about his drinking. I could not envision being a guest in someone's home and helping myself to their booze. I told him that I thought he had a problem. Later my daughter told me that he tried to get her to get out my drinks that I reserved for special holidays. Some bottles would last for years.

After this encounter I told my guest that I would help him find a place. Eventually I did. A construction man who had done some work for me lived alone. He offered a room and some work. My guest had a friend who was going to take him to the new place, but it never happened. So, I told him to get what he had together, and I would move him. The room worked out, but the work didn't. However, my construction friend would wake him up at 6:00 am encouraging him to find some work or another place.

Long story short. He did not stay long with my friend. But he found a job, found a place, and he is working to this day. Maybe he learned that if he dealt with the troubles of the day, the troubles of the tomorrows that became today would be much more manageable.

FOUR

CHILDREN – GOD'S KINGDOM – A SAFE PLACE

With my daughter in school and the boys in day care, my days became fairly normal. However, there were the evening nights, and weekends. I was pastoring a small church and doing some real estate. My life was pretty full. We were a family. As I think back, this had to be the most secure environment that the boys had experienced. One day I would come to know just how much my daughter was doing. I would learn to deeply respect a woman who was in school full-time or at work and raising children. I was in the house, but I did not see how much my daughter was doing.

In the evening she would cook a full meal for the boys. Sometimes I shared; however, although I will eat anything, I am pretty health conscious, when it comes to diet. She would clean up. I would spend some time with the boys. On cool evenings we would often build a fire by the creek. The boys loved it. We would take a stick with red coals on the end and write in the air when it was dark. They like to set off what I told them were mountain firecrackers. These were mountain laurel leaves. These green leaves would pop like small firecrackers. Sometimes we jumped on the trampoline which was not far from the fire.

While we played, Julia would clean the kitchen and spend time on homework. She was busy. When we came into the house, she would begin to get the boys ready for bath and bed. Many nights Julia would be up if one of the boys were sick. Jacques, the oldest, had asthmatic problems. Sometimes she would give him breathing treatments in the middle of the night.

I can see the boys now, playing on the swing set and slide or playing in the creek. I have a vivid picture of Jacques by the creek bank. I was weed-eating the bank. He asked me if I would cut a little further up the creek. He wanted to explore.

Jacques liked to take some water pipes that I had and use gravity flow to make a waterfall below. He could spend hours playing in the creek.

We have a low bridge to cross our creek. It was built with locust logs spaced in the creek. The space between the logs served as conduits for the water to flow through. Sometimes we would have water snakes on the bridge. They would disappear when the boys used the bridge as a kick-off for water play.

They would drop rocks into the water just to see the splash. They would send ships, boats or rafts through the bridge conduits and hurry to retrieve them on the lower side. Of course, they were not ships, or boats or rafts. They were whatever they imagined them to be. These boys were living in the moment. They were at peace. They trusted that their environment was safe.

Isaiah speaks about a place and a time when the whole world will be safe and at peace (see Is. 11:6-9). To these boys, at this young age, I myself symbolized tomorrow. Along with my daughter, we provided food, clothes, shelter, comfort, peace and love. For moments at a time, sometimes hours, they would travel to and explore in their child minds a world that slips away for most of us.

I remember pausing from some yard work. The boys were looking up the creek as if in wonder of how it just kept running. From throwing rocks to wading, to building dams, the boys reminded me of innocence in the first degree. Their minds, their souls and their heart seemed to be at unbelievable peace.

At times I would tell them about Isaiah 11:6-9. I know that Jacques believed what I told him because one day as we were finishing a shower, he asked "G-dad, what about sharks?" At first, I did not understand what Jacques was talking about. When I asked him what he meant, he said, "You know in Paradise." You see, Jacques believed the prophecy of Isaiah, and he wanted to know about sharks. I told him "Son you can probably hang on to its fin and ride on its back." This is our Daddy in heaven's reality that God himself brings to us.

I thought about the world that Isaiah prophesied about. In that writing Isaiah takes us to Paradise when he says in 11:6-9, "*the wolf will live with the lamb, the leopard will lie down with the goat, the calf and the lion and the yearling together; a little child will lead them. The cow will feed with the bear, their young will lie down together, and the lion will eat straw like an ox. The infant will play near the cobra's den and a young child will put its hand in the viper's nest. They will neither harm nor destroy on all my holy mountain, for the earth will be filled with the knowledge of the Lord as the waters cover the sea*". **My friends, that is paradise. Isaiah takes us back and forward at the same time!**

As we go back to Genesis following creation, God describes the food for all animals in Genesis 1:29, 30. It is plant life. Fruit, seeds, green plants. There is an assortment of food for humans and animals. There is no need to kill anything. Then there comes what we call the fall of humankind from God's rule to human rule. From the beginning, human beings were given the power of reasoning and free will. We can choose our way or God's way. Adam and Eve choose the way of humans which are in conflict with God's ways. Jesus, the new covenant maker, destroys the power of sin. Jesus leads us to see what he sees. For those who can grasp it and see it, Jesus is leading us to paradise and the garden of pleasure and delight (Eden). Through Jesus we get a do-over. Jesus restores us to a Daddy-child relationship with God. He leads us to a place in the kingdom of God where we can walk with God in the cool of the day.

The tender hearts of my boys often escaped into their own imagination. It is these tender hearts that God invites into his kingdom.

When we choose our way, we entered into the human journey which brings our lives into conflict with the ways of the devil against the ways of God. Our Father did not like to see Adam and Eve fearful of being seen naked, so God sacrificed the first animals. (See Genesis 3:21 which describes the garments of animal skin.)

This represents God's first sacrifice for his children. This would eventually lead to our Father's perfect sacrifice that had the love and the power of God to bring his children back into alignment with God Himself. Like a loving Father, he wants to wrap his arms around you and I and hold us close to his breast.

I had no idea what God was going to teach me through these boys. As I watched them grow and play in the beautiful innocence which they displayed, it took me back to an earlier time and place where I could play for hours with brothers and cousins. As children, we resided in the present. For us there was no time. We lived in wonder of life in the present.

JADEN AND GOD'S PEACE

I remember Jaden riding with me on the lawn mower. I had a comfortable seat, but Jaden would sit right on the steel at my feet on my

Scag-o-Turn mower. He would become comfortable and fall asleep. This reminds me of how my Father in heaven wants to be with me. His desire is to have the warmth of my heart at rest in his heart. His desire is to be with me now this moment and forever.

I must tell you about another comfort. Jaden was a natural at father-child comfort and peace. He is the younger of the two. I would take them both for walks in the woods. Some walks were really long. I was often giving the boys neck rides. Many times, Jaden would go limp. He would be on my neck, but he would become as limber as a rag. I would always make sure that I had a good hold on him. I can only imagine a little boy heart that feels totally secure, totally at peace and totally comfortable. No fear, no worries, no concern! This little boy would just melt into my care oblivious to everything around him. His body and heart received the warmth of total unconditional love. He moved into a place where he cast all fear away. He was in the hands of his G-dad. G-dad, being me, the grandfather by human standards. By little boy standards, I was the father of the present.

It is no wonder that Jesus says that you cannot enter the kingdom of heaven unless you become as a child. You cannot enter this kingdom by the will and purpose of human effort. To enter into this kingdom, you must be able to give all your fears, all your worries and all your concern into the loving heart of your Father (Daddy) who is in heaven.

You cannot accomplish this by human will and purpose. Jaden did not choose to place his heart into the safe keeping of G-dad. This was a result of a relationship that led him into a new realm of closeness. Jaden had received me. He trusted me! Without conscious decision, he loved me. This little boy was revealing what he had received from me. I believe that he knew in his heart that I would keep him safe and secure when he placed his care into my hands.

I must testify that my peace, comfort and security come when, like a little child, I place my trust in the hands of my Daddy in heaven. I envision the way my Father in heaven wants to carry me at times. Jaden, had turned over all cares to me. He felt safe. He felt secure. He trusted me. He knew that I loved him. In his heart he believed that I would take care of him. So, when we were close, Jaden just melted into that closeness.

Long ago my Dad took me hunting on a cold morning. All I know is that I was very young. It was very cold. My feet were hurting. My dad opened up his coat enough so that my legs and feet were practically in his coat. What a beautiful warmth it was. I became toasty warm and comfortable. I felt secure. I was loved and I trusted that love.

DADDY!

One evening I was in my carport. I could hear the stream below. There was no moon. Darkness was all around. I walked onto the patio. Without contemplation, without thought, I looked up to heaven. I saw the stars in their entire splendor. My mouth opened and my heart spoke, and across my lips came the word. This word came from the identification of my heart as to who I was speaking too. It was a revelation. My life suddenly and without warning moved into a new realm of existence. The word that came from my heart and across my lips was Daddy. I began to weep as I felt a new closeness, a greater trust, and a greater love. How can one better describe this than a small child in its parent's arms, comfortable, warm, toasty and secure?

Another way to describe this connection is an infant nursing at its mother's breast. For the infant, its identity is in the mother. From the infant's standpoint, they see their life in the mother. A born-again person begins to see their life in God.

It can't be emphasized enough; Jesus says that you must be born again before you can see the Kingdom of Heaven. He also says that you cannot enter the Kingdom of Heaven unless you become as a little child. Have you been born of God (Jn. 1:13)?

Life experiences can wound your heart, soul, mind and spirit, or it can strengthen your heart, mind, soul and spirit. Whether your strength overpowers the wounds of life is directly dependent upon how you respond to those experiences in life.

We all have them, ghosts of the past. Were they Casper the friendly ghost or were they demons? Maybe they were some of both. Do they offer freedom; or do they imprison your mind? Are they comfort, peace and joy with a dash of trust?

You should not want to look at your experiences from the adult point of view. You must see them with the innocence of a child. How was the child in you molded into the person that you are today? Which ghost dominates your life? Is it Casper or the ghost of hell?

JACQUES

One day I was going for a walk in the woods as I often do. Jacques wanted to go with me. So, my time became our time. I decided to go up the mountain behind my house on an old trail that had grown over. It was no longer a trail but followed along a small stream. The beginning started off up an embankment where the water flowed over large rocks. Some jetted out of the mountain where the stream rushed down to the drainpipe under the road.

We had not gone far before Jacques asked to ride on my neck. I relented. After all, this would make it a more serious workout for me. The trail was often encumbered, so I would get into the stream walking on the rock. Underneath, I am sure it was a mountain of rock. Many or most mountain streams flow just above the mountain core.

What I like about this walk is the huge rock displayed here and there. Some were as big as a dump truck with much diversity of appearance. Jacques rode effortlessly on my shoulders. Remember, Jacques is the oldest. Suddenly, Jacques spoke up in a nervous tone. He said, "Let's go home."

Even today my daughter tells me that his favorite drawing is my home. He says, "I want to live at G-dad's house." What is he really saying? Is he saying G-dad's is a place of peace, comfort and joy? Maybe for Jacques it just happened to be a place where he experienced having a heart that, without thought, trusted the environment and warmth a small child needs in order to feel secure.

Jacques had experienced a volatile relationship between his mom and dad. Because of substance abuse, he found himself moved from place to place in very unhealthy environments. His experiences contained wounds and ghosts of the past that left his little mind less secure and possibly fearful with an inability to trust completely like his younger brother Jaden.

"G-dad! Let's go home." Jacques had looked around at the forest. For him this trail did not appear to be a real trail that would lead us home. Everything looked the same - trees and rocks and a small stream. Coach as I might to go a little further was an agitation to Jacques. Jacques (now eight years old) was about four at the time. I believe that, in his mind, he was lost. Why could he not completely trust me? Just maybe he had trusted before and that trust had placed this infant little boy mind in a place or places of internal terror. How many times had this little boy's heart been wounded? That day I realized that though the egg and the sperm that brought Jacques and Jaden to life were from the same parents, Jacques and Jaden's experiences were different. Jacques had experienced a more uncertain life than his younger brother Jaden. The wounds were deeper for Jacques, and on the trail this day, fear overpowered trust. As I encouraged Jacques to go with me a little further, tears welled up in his eyes. The thief (Satan) had robbed a little boy of some of his ability to trust.

My friends, when we allow the enemy of humanity to rob a little child, we are allowing the forces of evil to over-shadow the light of life.

I wanted to go further but the idea brought terror to my little boy. I relented and we headed home. I can even now hear his voice when he said, "There it is!" With the foliage off the trees, he caught a glimpse of the roof top of our home. I reached up and pulled him down so that I could look into his face. When that boy smiles, it is broad and wide and his eyes gleam. Even now this minute I want to hold this little boy close and give him a big hug. My friend, do not wait until tomorrow.

Today is yesterday's tomorrow. Hug that little child today. For me, today is a tomorrow that places that little boy hundreds of miles away. We never know what days, weeks and months may bring. Capture the magic of this day. We do not know how quickly it will slip away. Cherish that smile. Cherish that embrace. Cherish that fellowship. One day it will just be a memory. One day that child will no longer be a child and he may be far away, and all you have is yesterday's memories. Today is the day for our children to experience love, peace, joy, comfort and trust.

SORROW – LOVE - ABUNDANCE

It amazes me that so much pain and sorrow come from the investment of true, pure, unconditional love. Scripture tells us that Jesus is a man of much sorrow, suffering and pain. If we never loved, we would never experience the passing of a loved one, because we would not have loved them. It would be just a passing. It is because we love that we experience the pain of separation. Jesus teaches us to always be thankful (1 Thes. 5:18).

Why would we be instructed to be thankful in all things? You can find this instruction in 1 Thessalonians 5:19. To get a deeper meaning, read 5:12-28. This instruction is for all people. However, to be able to grasp this and fully understand it, you must be born of God (Jn. 1:13). People born of God have entered into a new realm of existence that enables them to more fully understand the abundance that God has sent humanity in the person of Jesus.

There are two verses in Luke 21:16 and 18. These verses contain messages where one statement from Jesus seems to be in opposition with the other. Humanly speaking, they are. On a deeper level they are in complete harmony with the words of Jesus in the gospel of John chapter six verse sixty-three. Here Jesus says in response to eating his body and drinking his blood; *"The Spirit gives life; the flesh counts for nothing. The words I have spoken to you, they are full of the Spirit and life."*.

Let us go now to the two verses in Luke 21:16, 18. One verse deals with death. The other verse deals with life. Jesus was speaking to his disciples when he said, *"some of you will be put to death."* Here Jesus is speaking about their temporary existence. We are all living in the flesh and are living under the sentence of death. Death is a fearful thing for the human mind whose confidence is in the flesh. Like Jesus says in the long run or short for that matter, "*it counts for nothing.*" However, when we look at verse :18, Jesus says "*not a hair of your head will perish.*" This is our eternal existence.

Jesus says that before you can enter the kingdom of heaven you must become like a little child (see Mat. 18:3). I think of Jaden who could go limp as a rag riding on my neck. He was in my care, and he knew in his heart that his life was safe. He trusted.

Jesus also told Nicodemus that he could not see the kingdom of heaven unless he was born again or born of God. Nicodemus knew that this was a human impossibility. Jesus wanted to bring Nicodemus to a new level of existence. Jesus was talking about a new permanent life verses a temporary life. Through our human eyes, we cannot see a forever life. You and I can begin to see our eternity when we are born into a new life with our Daddy in heaven.

Children are born with the God given ability to trust. However, at every turn possible, in life there is a thief who wants to rob each child of trust. Jaden trusted me completely because of his experience with me. The thief had not yet robbed him. Jacques, on the other hand, had experienced enough uncertainty in his life that complete trust was elusive.

There are as many different experiences as there are people. That is why my teacher, the Holy Spirit, teaches me not to judge another human being. Neither am I to condemn others. The apostle John writes that God did not send Jesus into the world to condemn the world. So, if God's purpose is not to condemn, how could anyone who says that they follow Jesus judge or condemn anyone? For God loved the world and you and I so much that he gave his one and only Son into the sorrows of hell so we may see the light of life in Jesus.

God teaches pure, sweet love. My boys are very young. We could say that their life is just beginning. However, a lot of seeds have already been planted in their lives.

Some days it seemed that Jaden would push a toy lawn mower for hours. As I watched him, I wondered what was going on in that little-boy mind. What I did not realize at the time was what was happening in my mind and my relationship with the boys. A revelation was taking place before my eyes, and I was completely unaware of what God would teach me.

I loved my daughter and the boys. However, I did not realize that as I gave, I was receiving. I was giving love. It was the Godkind of love. I gave with no requirements that it would be returned. However, as my heart loved more, my Father in heaven poured more of his love into my heart.

Human beings who are made in the image of God are actually made to love. Pure unadulterated love is what completes us. It is truly the desire of our hearts to love and be loved. What we are able to give is based on what we have received. What this means to me is that my ability to love is in alignment with my ability to receive love. We do not truly love as a conscious effort. As I watched Jaden with the toy mower or Jacques working with the pipe using gravity flow to create a waterfall, my heart was being fed. Love was happening. Without effort my fondness for the boys was growing. They were becoming the apples of my eye. God was doing something.

What God was doing was smiling as the apples of his eye were growing in love. Yet, with love comes pain. There is a risk when you love. You may be hurt and rejected. Love will often bring pain, suffering and sorrow. Isaiah prophesied many things about Jesus.

Although Jesus was in the beginning, the world has only come to know about him over these last two thousand plus years.

Isaiah says about Jesus in 53:11, *"After he has suffered, he will see the light of life and be satisfied."* Why did Jesus have to suffer? The answer is love. Our Daddy in heaven loves us. So, God gave us Jesus to right the wrong. Satan, the thief, cunningly robbed Adam and Eve, who were created in the image of God. They were like God. They were God's creation. However, Satan convinced them that they were missing out on something.

Paraphrasing, the devil told Eve, "Check out this tree. Oh, how delicious this fruit appears. God knows that if you eat this fruit, you will be like him. Take a bite. It will bring you to a new level. You will be like God." (See Gen. 3:1-5 for Eve's discussion with the serpent). Wait a minute! When I read Genesis 1:26, 27, I am told that Eve was created in God's image. So, she was already like God. Adam and Eve's problem seemed to be their innocence. They are in the wrong company, and they do not know it.

The worse thing is that Adam and Eve do not seem to know who they are. When Jesus came to right the wrong, he was tempted in the wilderness. Jesus knew who he was. He was God's Son. Adam and Eve were also God's children. Their true identity would be revealed in them only if they truly came to understand who they were.

The message that Jesus brought to all humanity is that to become all that we can, we must first know who we are. When we can identify who we are in God, then we can see our eternal reality in the realm of God's kingdom. Until we see this new, born-again person, we are trapped in this temporal body of flesh that will cease to exist.

The boys and I were growing in love together. It was not a plan. There was no thought about it. This growing love had a life of its own. It was happening as naturally as breathing. How does it happen? First of all, we are made in the image of Love. Our Daddy made us in his image and his likeness. Every human being has the attributes of God. He created us from his creation. That is the earth. Every person even now is created from the dust of the earth. Every sperm and egg come into being because the man and woman feed off the earth.

We can see the food that we eat. However, we cannot see love. Love is truly a wondrous substance, but it cannot be seen. When Phillip said to Jesus, "*Show us the Father*," Jesus responded, "*Don't you know me?*". Jesus went on to say to Phillip that if you have seen Jesus, you have seen the Father. Humanly speaking this is a very strange statement. However, when I see from my heart the chemistry, the electricity and the love flowing between me and the boys, it is the unseen substance of love that has spiritual and eternal implications. Jesus says that his words are full of the Spirit and life. For Jesus and those who follow him, the motivation is love.

YOU ARE BORN TO LOVE

We are born to love. You are born to give love. My boys and I did not know that we were receiving and giving love. As the adult when I was with the boys, it was good and profitable to make a decision. Were they with me, or, was I with them? This decision is important. It can create a mood of tension as we try to get children to do what we want, or it can be more freeing and relaxing as you let them lead. When you let them lead, you become a guide for their benefit and protection. As much as possible, you give them the freedom to set the agenda.

When you are with them, you will discover that they want to be with you. They want your security and your protection. I can see each of the boys looking back at me as they attempt to extend their limits as if to say, "Is it o.k. for me to climb this tree? Can I go out on the limb and hang down? Will you catch me if I fall? Or will you catch me if I turn loose, or if I jump?" In these encounters, in all of them something invisible is flowing through the air. It is an unseen substance. It is a bonding agent. The bond of love is growing.

LOVE WILL NOT RETURN VOID

Asking to know Jesus more personally, more intimately, and more passionately is asking to know love in a greater degree. I believe that we all, (or at least most of us,) have felt the power of love. How can you explain it? How does it grow?

Jesus says some of the craziest things. Give and you will receive. How does giving become receiving? Sometimes your gift of love, friendship or acceptance is not received. You love, you are a friend, and you accept the other person for who they are. Yet, your gifts are rejected. How then do you receive? *"Give and it will be given to you. A good measure, pressed down, shaken together and running over, will be poured into your lap. For with the measure you use, it will be measured to you."* (Luke 6:38).

In the language of God, you will find that you give out from the abundance you have received. I did not love my boys because they were perfect or because they always responded to me in a positive manner. These boys were beautiful. Yet, at times they exhibited the Cain and Abel syndrome. They would be jealous of one another, and they would fight. I loved them just because God has loved me without measure or condition. My Daddy's love is genuinely true love. It is like a seed planted in your heart. The fertilizer is in the giving. A natural law takes effect. When love is poured out of you,

you have no less love to give. As you love, your abundance of love will grow like a plant in fertile soil being watered by the Father in heaven.

Jesus says that to see him is to see the Father. Jesus is asking Phillip to see him with the eyes of his heart. Jesus is teaching his followers God's reality of life. Jesus wants his follower to see the true bond that binds them together. That bond is love.

I could have said, "Woe is me," when Julia showed up with the boys. I do not believe that I reacted any certain way. Maybe I was thinking, "This is temporary." "Who knows what my daughter will do next?" I had no idea what God was doing. However, I had asked to know Jesus more personally, more intimately, and with a greater passion. At the time, I had no thought that over the next few years I would come to know love at a deeper level.

It is important for all of us to realize that our journey in life is just that - a journey. I have often thought about how wonderful it would have been to have been more deeply involved with God when I began a family, to be truly free to love in the power of God. I must...I say that I must forgive myself for who I was.

I am not saying that I was a bad person. It is just that Satan had robbed me when I began a family. While serving in Vietnam, I had man's version of God. I had a religious version of the character of God. When I began to question God, I questioned the god that I had received based upon my experiences and teachings concerning the identity of God. Please do not get me wrong, there were many good intentions. However, the cunning of the devil had created confusion about God. In John 9:24b the religious leaders judge God to be a sinner while at the same time counting themselves to be agents of God. Listen to these people who claim to represent God. They say, *"Give glory to God by telling the truth. We know this man is a sinner"* (Jn. 9:24b). This man is Jesus, the Son of God, the Messiah, God with us.

In my first marriage I was a man of unbelief and denied that God even existed. I have heard of hate and rage among soldiers of war. I did not have rage. I did not hate my enemies and I had a natural God-given compassion for the common people of Vietnam. They were caught in the middle of a war which I doubt they understood.

Most of the people were farmers, which means rice growers. Most of their homes were on hard-packed, swept clean dirt floors. Their homes were primarily bamboo framing and rice straw for the roof and siding. I have witnessed them cooking with a small flame of rice straw.

Their work animals are water buffalo.

LIFE'S JOURNEY CREATES YOUR IDENTITY

Six years before I went to Vietnam I went to live with my grandparents. This was part of the molding of my character. We lived in an old frame house. I could see light through the walls of my bedroom. There was a total of six light bulbs in the entire house. It had a metal roof that sometimes leaked. Our heat and our cook stove were wood burning. All water had to be carried from a stream about three hundred yards below the house. Wash day was a challenge! We had an outhouse. Sponge baths were the norm. A weekly tub bath was costly. In the summer we could bathe in the creek.

The reason the tub baths were costly was because they required a fire to heat the water. Wood had to be cut and split. Water had to be carried. My friends, when I turn on the water, I know that there is a cost. When I turn on hot water, the cost goes up. I have experienced the cost in a way that most people today cannot identify with. If we ate, we prepared soil, planted, plowed (with a horse), and weeded.

We fed the horse, the cow, the hogs and the chickens from what we grew. I identified with these people in Vietnam who farmed the land. When I saw a peasant plowing with a water buffalo, I could visualize my grandfather or myself behind a big black work horse named Trigger. This horse was a well-trained work horse. He would move right when you spoke the word "gee," or left when you said "haaw". At the end of a row of corn, without command he would turn into the next row. My job with the plow was to guide it through the middle of the row so that the plow would place soil around the stalks of corn. At the same time, I would be plowing up the weeds between the rows. Someone with a hoe would follow behind for the final touch.

The corn was the main substance. It was grain for the horse, the cow, the pigs, the chickens and it was the source of our cornbread. The corn came from the soil which fed the horse to work the fields and haul the wood. The corn fed the cow who gave the milk for drinking and for butter. It fed the pigs that became the ham, the bacon, the sausage and more. The corn also fed the chickens that laid the eggs and became fried chicken.

The work horse had a heavy load. It plowed the fields and the garden. It pulled the mower that cut the hay and the rake that raked the hay into piles. The horse pulled the wagon that hauled the corn and the hay. We hauled the corn to the grain mill to be ground into chops for the cow and meal for cornbread. Chops were the corn with the shucks and the cob grown together. As you can see, the horse was a very important animal for a small rural farm.

I have said all of the above to help you understand who I am. We are all the sum of our experiences multiplied together. It is our journey in life that molds our identity.

I have said that I have heard of soldiers who allow fear to turn to anger, hate and rage. All of these factors and more serve to separate us from our true identity, which is found in the One who created us. That means that I was created in the image of God (see Gen. 1:26, 27). However, humanity is seeking its own image. When Adam and Eve decided to seek their own image apart from God, they stepped into a flawed image of who they were created to be. When Satan tempted them, they could not resist the idea or the concept of becoming their own god (see Gen. 3:1-7).

Jesus was sent to us to reveal the true image of God. He was sent to null and void the destructive power of the devil that was in the humanity that seeks to be their own god.

Let us return to the Vietnam farmers and family. As I looked upon them, I could see the struggle. I could see smiling but troubled children living in the uncertainty of a war-torn country. I could identify with the farmers. The men, the women and the children all worked. I can only imagine the lives of families who once lived in the vacant huts and homes. What happened? Man happened! War happened! Evil happened!

When I witnessed our huge tanks, amtracks and other machinery driving through maturing rice paddies, I cringed. I knew that one day the soil had been plowed. The seed had been planted. The crop had been worked. The harvest would be soon. We drove over these crops without any idea or understanding that these crops meant life to a family.

Once riding shotgun with a truck driver, I was with a driver who sought, without knowledge, to turn friends into enemies. On the road he swerved intentionally to hit the ends of bamboo sticking out the end of a long cart. The cart was like a light-weight wagon which was pulled by the laborer. This cart was loaded with long bamboo which could be used for framing or fencing. The laborers seem to be cleaning up after a hard day's work in the water or a rice paddy. In a few seconds, the careless driver had damaged many hours of labor. I can still see the anxiety of the man as he threw his hands up and shrunk in disbelief. I felt his pain. I had compassion for him. I will have more later about my experiences in Vietnam but for now, back to my boys.

The infant breathes life-giving oxygen into its lungs. When you are born of God, like the infant's first inhalation, you receive the life of Christ into your being. That is, you receive God into your life, and are born of God. A transition is taking place as you move from the temporary life of flesh into an eternal being born of God.

BORN OF GOD

When the infant has breathed in, the infant must exhale before it can take in more air. For the born-again person exhaling is releasing your old temporal life to God so that you can receive more of God into your life. The natural law of God begins to take effect. The more of your temporal life that you give to God, the more of the life of Christ you receive. Therefore, it is the giving that becomes the receiving.

As you are being transformed, God's law of giving is the catalyst of his love. You receive God's love. You return God's love to him and his creation. As you begin to pour love out of your life to others, God's love becomes a fountain of love within you. It is gushing up in you. You give it away and it flows more abundantly into you and through you. Your life becomes God's kingdom of love that is within you. You are a new child born of God. When you allow God's love to fill you, God will give you a love that will spill out from you as you journey through this life.

What is happening is that God's image of himself now has a home within you. God's kingdom is there. What an awesome privilege it is to be an instrument of love that is wider than the earth and deeper than the seas.

How could I possibly know how deeply God would touch me through my boys? I have found that it is the innocence of a child's love that is true and pure. It is like God's love.

Julia began to bring the boys to a little church that I was privileged to pastor. We were a growing ministry. Jaden got into the "amens" and "hallelujahs". The boys brought a new kind of life to the ministry. They could be beautiful, or they could be little devils. However, they were always true to their feelings. I remember our fellowship time as they would run and play. They were touching hearts in a way that was impossible for me.

I do not know why I keep getting this picture of Jacques climbing a tree. The real picture is after he had climbed up the tree. He was smiling. His mouth was so wide that I could see almost all of his teeth. His eyes were bright. He was beautiful. My heart is still warmed as my mind goes back to those moments of giving and receiving. For Jacques, it was a gift that I allowed him to climb. When he would look at me with that broad smile, there was also a question in his mind. Is it ok if I climb? He would climb and without saying a word, he was saying "Look at me." Sometimes he would hang down and ask me to catch him. Sometimes I would. Other times I would say, "It is ok you can drop. It is not too far."

It was impossible for me to know what was happening in all of our lives. My daughter has told me (more than once) that Jacques' favorite drawing is G-dad's house. For a child, it is a wonderland. Creeks and ponds to play in, a low bridge to float things under, rocks to skip, dams to build, a complete swing set (it is big), hills to descend on skateboards, deep walks into the woods, campfires and more.

The campfires were an event unto themselves – marshmallows, s'mores, hot dogs and drawing in the dark night through the air with sticks. There were the mountain firecrackers, mountain laurel leaves that would exhibit numerous popping sounds when thrown into a hot fire.

Our fires were built beside active streams that had their own everchanging voices. The water was a cascade flowing over rock and two to six-foot waterfalls near our home. The waters were like the boys. They were always changing, and they spoke in many voices. They spoke in gurgles and in their landings after a fall into pools of water below. Sometimes they came rushing down, moving rock and debris out of their way.

We once dug a pool about a foot and a half deep. Nice for wading and playing. However, the waters came rushing down in torrents and filled it higher than before with rock and sand. My boys were like the waters and the creek beds. They were forever changing.

You cannot open-heartedly participate with young boys in this atmosphere without changing. Even now, I have the vision in my mind of smiles and bright eyes. It is one thing to share in these events through the eyes of an adult, but quite another through the eyes of a child.

It is the eyes of each child based on their perception of life. Was it a big fire or was it real big or small? How warm or how hot is it?

I did not know, at the time, that God through the Spirit of truth was teaching me to see his very own heart in myself. He was taking a scalpel to my heart. I did not even know that he was peeling away the human heart so that I could receive his heart.

A SCALPEL TO MY HEART

My desire for the well-being of my boys was undeniable. I hurt when they hurt. I laughed with them. I comforted them when they were hurt or afraid. I knew that I would give my life for them. They were mine and, for a time, they were entrusted into my keeping.

I believe and know that my God is absolutely amazing. I did not know what was happening as my Daddy in heaven began to reveal his heart in me. As he did so, God himself brought my heart into his heart. I began to experience love in a way that I never thought possible. As God gave me his heart for these boys, it was not for them alone. It was for all humanity. It was a new kind of love, but it was personal for me. I know now that God created me and all of humanity with a heart to reflect his image in which we are all created. When God lives in you, unconditional love and forgiveness also lives in you.

What happened when Satan seduced Adam and Eve is that the human race was damaged? The conflict of life that followed was humanity's desire to be their own god. The human heart began to be in conflict with God's heart.

Now we are dealing with two hearts. The human heart and the heart of God. The human heart ends in death. God's heart in you is life in abundance and eternal. The human heart has been led into darkness. God's heart is light and life. The human heart falls prey to lies and deceit. God's heart is full of the truth. We do not need to balance these two hearts. What must happen is cutting out the dying human heart and replacing it with God's heart, but we ourselves cannot do it.

As human beings we are trapped in a dying body. We cannot do anything to change this. However, God can, if we are willing to die to the ways of the flesh. When Jesus came, He was a reflection of who we are meant to be. In his personhood, we see God. In his heart, we see a great undeniable love for all humanity. It is not love as we know love, humanly speaking.

Religion has put a name on God's love in trying to describe it as different. Until we can experience God's love as different, a name for his love has no value. Jesus describes this love best when he says that there is no greater love than to give your life because of that love. The power of God is that Jesus is love. The love of God revealed in Jesus is never in the past tense.

God's love is not bound by space and time. It simply is. My boys simply are. For them the past is gone, but the future is out of reach. They live life in the present. What we are doing this minute is the only minute that we have control over. We can't borrow a minute from the past any more than we can reach into the future to borrow a minute to extend one of our most glorious moments.

Even as I write, I cannot bring the past to the present, and I can only anticipate my next encounter with the boys. However, I can bask in memories that flood my mind and touch my heart.

FIVE

BAD NEWS; GOOD NEWS; YOU JUDGE

Julia and the boys had been with me only a few months when I discovered that Julia was pregnant. Julia had entered Tri-County College and was pursuing a business degree. She was also taking other classes of cosmetology. She hoped to have her own business. So, she was busy. However, she had become pregnant and now had a greater burden of caring for another child. She continued to work hard. She handled the pregnancy quite well.

She kept her classes up and cooked and cleaned for the boys. One day I would come face to face with just how much she was doing. For the moment, let me just say that my hat is off to a mother who takes good care of her children, and those moms in school or working. It is nothing less than double duty!

One day I had prayed to know Jesus more intimately. Realizing what I said, I immediately prayed for mercy. I have also come to realize that to know Jesus is to experience suffering and sorrow. They go hand in hand with God's love which brings a new and beautiful joy into the heart of the receiver.

As I mentioned earlier, neither you nor I can give of God until we have received from God. Human beings do not have the God-capacity to love until they have received God's love revealed in Jesus into themselves. If you have not received it, you do not have it to give.

We all have a natural human capacity to love. However, when Adam and Eve were disobedient to God in the garden, our ability to love was damaged. Until that damage is repaired, you cannot give and receive love in its total beauty and passion. When you have received the power of Jesus' love, it is this love that gives you the ability to love as God loves.

What was God doing with this sixty-five-year-old child (me) when he turned my life upside down with a daughter who has two boys less than four years old and is now pregnant? To make matters worse all my eggs were in the real estate market, and that market was in the worst slump that I had witnessed since 1971 (the year I entered into real estate). The year Julia moved in was 2011.

What was God doing? Was he doing something to me or for me? As it has turned out my Daddy in heaven was teaching me to see my boys as he sees me. God himself was creating within me a new heart. He revealed his heart to me, and I received it. My Father became my Daddy while I became the boys G-dad.

Just as the boys were touching me, I was touching God. God began to flow through our lives like a river. He gave. I gave. And he gave more. As the boys began to identify their life in me, I began to see my life in God. Jesus' words, *"I am in the Father and the Father is in me,"* was becoming a reality. I began to see Jesus in me and me in Jesus. Jesus said that we cannot enter the kingdom of heaven unless we become as a little child.

My little grandson Jacques believed without question the paradise of God and God's heaven which Jesus is preparing for those who love him. I told Jacques about Isaiah 11:6-9. These verses paint a beautiful picture of the place where Jesus is leading those who are following him. These words are more than words. In God's reality we can only begin to see this vision coming to pass when we have been born of God. When we are born of God, Jesus takes us into God's eternal Kingdom.

Remember, the human mind is damaged material. That damage can only be repaired by God. What does God do? He sends us Jesus who is fully human and fully God. Jesus was born of Mary, a woman of flesh; therefore, Jesus became as we are so that we may become as he is.

Becoming as Jesus must be accomplished by the power of God. This is an impossible task for any human. That which is temporary cannot make or become that which is eternal. When I told Jacques about Isaiah 11:6-9, Jacques believed me. I can see this vision as a reality:

"The wolf will live with the lamb, the leopard will lie down with the goat, the calf and the lion and the yearling together, and a little child will lead them. The cow will feed with the bear, their young will lie down together, and the lion will eat straw like the ox. The infant will play near the Cobra's den, and the young child will put its hand into the viper's nest. They will neither harm nor destroy on all my holy mountain; for the earth will be filled with the knowledge of the Lord as the waters cover the sea" (Isaiah 11:6-9).

Now think about Isaiah 11:6-9. Do you believe? Can you see it? Jacques could see it. I know that he could see it. Why could he see it? When I told him, I spoke with not just my tongue and lips. I spoke with my heart. I could see it and the wind of the truth was blowing. Jesus said, *"You cannot see this wind. You do not know where it comes from or where it goes."* (Jn. 3:8). Jesus was talking about the Spirit.

How can I know that Jacques believed it? The Spirit confirmed it. One evening we were getting out of the shower. This shower has a high step over ledge to get in. It has a shower head on each side, and it can be filled to over two feet. At the time, we were draining it as we were preparing to dry before getting out. I do not know where Jacques' question came from. I do not remember speaking about Isaiah at the time. Jacques asked the question as if we had been currently discussing the subject.

There was a conversation going on in his mind that I was not aware of. Out of the blue (but not really) he asked; "G-daddy what about sharks?" I asked. "What about them, Jacques?" "You know," he said. I said, "Son, I do not know. What are you thinking about?" "What about sharks in heaven?" he asked. I said with total confidence, "Son you can probably hold on to their fin and ride on their back."

That statement satisfied Jacques. The wind blows my friends. What kind of wind is blowing over your children? And, when I say your children, I am speaking about all children that you are given the opportunity to tell the good news of Jesus "The Christ" in a way by which a child can receive the vision of God's eternity. The development of a new mind and a new heart can begin at any time, at any age.

I believe that the Spirit of truth intervened in the heart and mind of little Jacques. Later, after the boys had moved to live with their dad, the boys would come on a visit. They would readjust right back into the swing of things.

MUD IS BEAUTIFUL

Another time while the boys were with me, we had heavy rains. I felt like it was a good time to check on my road ditches. I have over a mile of roads. It was still drizzling and very wet. I came to a place where the water had pushed from underneath the surface a large chunk of the road bank. I could see that a little shoveling could correct the drainage. This earth movement was at a hard-left turn that continued on an upgrade. With the drainage correction the road would be wider and the turn easier, so I set to work shoveling dirt and mud. The boys loved being out in this nature. The weather was warm but wet.

As they began to play in the water, they would look back at me to see if I was going to scold them. When I did not scold them, Jaden ventured a little further with a few stomps in the muddy water. When I jumped into the play, it was on. I knew that we would all be a mess. However, playing in the water on this muddy bank brought joy to these boys.

Jaden is the one who stands out in my mind. He would jump, splash, and stomp. He would then look back at me. I smile just thinking about it. I can see his face light up. I can see his eyes, his teeth, and face with a joyous smile. He is smiling. However, his expression has a question. I wish that I could have gotten into his mind. This is what I think that he was thinking:

"Is this really ok? When is G-dad going to get mad and scold me?" After a little pause, Jaden grinned as his eyes lit up and he jumped into the muddy water.

I like to think that little boy wounds were being healed as we played on muddy banks and in the ditch. The water oozed out of the bank enough to make a small stream. When we built the roads, we had probably interrupted an underground flow of water that happened during heavy rains.

The earth in itself is clean, even when it is wet and muddy. God created it all. However, too often we lose that child-like mentality that says mud is fun. You cannot find an experience with mud and water in a water park. I could say "sanitized" water park. The truth is that muddy bank and ditch were probably cleaner than a park with hundreds or thousands of people sharing the same water.

A BABY IS BORN

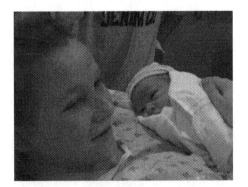

Julia's pregnancy had moved along naturally, and the time came for Julia to give birth to her third boy. A helpless, innocent child was born. A newborn child's image is closely tied to the mom. The innocent baby sees its life in the mother. To the newborn, the mother is its life.

This is her first birth that I was not present for. I do not remember the details. I guess that I was caring for Jacques and Jaden. I remember visiting the hospital, but I do not remember anything special about the visit. Julia was wrapped up in names. There is absolutely no way that I could see what was taking place in the realm of God's kingdom.

God was adding to his recipe of love, but who could see it? Julia came home with Sean and now our household was five. At least, there were five that could be seen. However, the wind of the Spirit was at work like a master craftsman.

Life became pretty normal with a single daughter and three boys. Normal was a baby crying at night. My daughter seemed to be up in the middle of every night. Looking back, I do not know how she kept up, but she did.

Sean was born October 5, 2012. Julia and Sean were the hit of our family gathering which was usually the week before Christmas.

This tradition began with my Mom prior to 1975. When exactly, I do not know. However, I do remember my sister's phone call late at night after I had gone to bed on Christmas Eve. When I answered the phone, it wasn't "I hate to be calling this late." It wasn't "how are you?" The conversation started with a question. The question was, "When are you going to be here?" I got up. My ex-wife got up. Then we got John, Edward and Dianna up. When I married Lorraine, she had three children. They became our children. James and Julia came later, giving us five children total. We drove about twenty-seven miles to my mom's. That year, I knew without a doubt that a tradition was established.

As far back as I can remember family traditions were always a big part of my life. Sure, they have changed over the years. However, family gatherings have always been, and continue to be, a big part of my life. Traditions add to life. They enrich life and add meaning. Our gatherings continue and it is my desire that my boys become part of our tradition.

Julia and the boys, along with myself, settled into a pretty normal life considering the circumstances. At least, at this time, the boys were in a stable environment. Through the winter, we had regular fires in the wood heater. That wasn't enough for the boys. They liked campfires behind the house. The fires were a regular thing.

My memory up to this point about Sean is a little fuzzy. However, Jacques and Jaden were always in the picture. They wanted to help cut and carry wood. Jaden stands out in this area. I think that it was because of his age. I would find him trying to cut wood with the axe. This was a safety concern but fortunately he never got hurt. That boy when carrying wood would make me think of an ant. He carried some mighty big sticks of wood for a two-year-old.

A LOST BOY - JADEN

One day during a noon day bible study, the church phone kept ringing. Since we were rarely there, I figured it was a sales call or wrong number. After the third or fourth time one of the ladies insisted that we answer the phone. Thank God, we did. It was my daughter. She was in panic mode. Jaden was missing. I asked her if she had looked in our ponds and creeks. She had. Having creeks and ponds are great! However, they are a concern when you have toddlers who have not reached a point in their life to fear anything. Jaden had always been protected and, therefore, had no fear.

To illustrate his fearlessness, I digress to an earlier incident. One day I was doing some work near one of the ponds. I was on my tractor. I was allowing Jaden to play just below where I was working. I did not want him to get close to the work area, so my eyes were always looking to see what he was doing. He was on our driveway near the entrance to our house. Without warning he took off running in that toddler fashion. He was leaning slightly forward almost in perfect run form. It wasn't unusual for him to run, but this time I knew exactly where he was headed. I had to get the tractor stopped safely. Engage the brake, and then exit quickly so that I could reach Jaden and the edge of the pond. In his little boy mind, he must have thought that what he was looking at might be a neat place to play. I had immediately shifted into high gear, but he got to the edge of the pond before I could reach him. He did not stop at the pond edge. He kept going. As soon as he hit the shallow water, he went down face first. Within a second, I had him picked up. Can you imagine that little boy mind? To him, the pond was inviting. He had no fear.

Back to the phone call! Jaden was missing. She had checked all water areas and every crevice around the house. She had called 911. By the time I got home, she had neighbors, first responders and deputies all over the place. I asked a neighbor what areas they had covered. In less than a minute I was up a ridge with thick underbrush. At his shorter height Jaden could walk under what I had to work my way through. When I got to the top of the ridge, I came out on a road that I had cut into my property. I was a good distance up the mountain. I surmised that there was no way a toddler could have gotten this far.

As the time passed, I became more and more uneasy. I was afraid that he might have gone to the road. There, he could have been abducted by one of the most dangerous creatures on earth. a human being! On the other hand, we had bears and coyotes. I knew that bears were less dangerous than a pack of coyotes. Animals in a pack could be dangerous, especially to a small child.

THE SUN IS GOING DOWN!

I headed down the roadbed. I hadn't gone far until I came upon Jaden's mittens and toboggan. In this late winter (March) afternoon, the sun had warmed up this mountain climbing toddler. I knew then that the evidence proved that this little boy had, in fact gotten, this far and further. I headed back up the road. There was a sharp left curve near the end. My daughter Julia and the sheriff's deputy had checked out the road. The deputy asked me to stay where I was for observation so that he and Julia could search further up the mountain. There were probably more than twenty people engaged in the search. However, Jaden's mom and I were desperate for results.

The sun had begun to sink. Even now on this east side of the mountain the sun no longer shone. Looking West I could see that the sun continued to bathe the earth. However, looking to the East, the sun was not visible. My heart was pounding.

I had walked this property numerous times. I knew the ups and downs. Coming up the mountain through the thickets I had proven that no one there could match my pace. I was deeply and desperately motivated.

Although I was older, I was and am a conditioned athlete. There is no way that I could stand still. That would be like giving a strong hunting dog a whiff of the prey, then tying it to a tree. I had found the mittens and the toboggan. G-dad was determined to find his boy. When the deputy said to stay there, it took about a three second discussion and I was in the woods calling as I moved, "Jaden, Jaden." That name was more than a name to me. At this moment in time I wanted, I needed, I desired to see the flesh and blood that that name represented. There was a quietness about him. There was a little child with a deep need to be held, and hugged, and loved. For a period of time, he was my boy. He was my child, and he probably did not even understand what it meant to be lost. He was innocent. He was lovely. He was beautiful, and I wanted to find him more than he wanted to be found. He was lost and didn't know it. He was lost and I knew it.

It is amazing what God will do to teach us and mold us into the image that we are created to be. However, the process cannot begin until our Daddy in heaven finds us. Another thing that amazes me is that we do not know that we are lost until we have been found. I am sure that Jaden could hear a lot of the commotion around our home and on the side of the mountain. He had no clue that it was all about him.

In my earlier personal rejection and denial of God, I had no clue that all along God was seeking to reveal himself in his true identity. He did not want me to see a god that was a figment of my experiences in life. This God of wonders wanted me to see and experience the true image of himself. A counterfeit god would one day be exposed as worthless. I know that a loving Father does not give what is worthless to his child any more than I would give worthless gifts to my boy Jaden.

Jaden was lost and he did not know it. I have been there. Jaden was waiting to be rescued but he did not know that he needed to be rescued. When God found me, I had no idea how lost I was. Jaden alone on a mountain and a cold night could have been fatal. My life without God would have been fatal.

The clock was ticking on the side of darkness. I waded through the brush without a conscious effort of breath or any inclination of pain or effort. I had seen his mittens and his toboggan. I sensed that he was somewhere close, but the woods were thick, and the shadows were falling. I was desperate because

I had a desperate kind of love for this boy. How can we understand this deep penetrating love that is more powerful than life itself?

Why was I desperate? My heart had been and is more deeply touched because of this one life. I have many loved ones. That is because I love. This love for Jaden didn't just happen or suddenly manifest itself deep inside me. This love had been and is being nurtured because of a relationship. This relationship of love was in my heart from before my physical existence. This love is placed in the human heart from the very beginning of human life. We are created in God's image (Gen. 2:26, 27). We are created to love. This love that so often rests in the human heart never completely blossoms into the kind of love which God created it to be. True love is obedient to God's love. Therefore, our hearts yearn to be at home with God, so we can experience love the way that it was originally intended to be. To be able to experience this love we must transcend our human existence. Like the apostle John writes, we must receive this love and believe in the source of this love before we are given the right to use its power to move into a dimension where there is no time. In this dimension, the eyes of our hearts are open to receive the kind of love that only God can give because it is a love that has no end. In the physical realm we cannot comprehend the eternal. So, we must move.

The only way I can explain it is that we are created to love. We are made in the image of love. When God gave us His Son, the Son was given in the power of love. The apostle John says, "*for God so loved the world that he gave us his Son*" (Jn. 3:16 paraphrase). His Son would teach us that love is more powerful than death. He would teach us that love had conquered death. Love has conquered fear and we are created in the image of God's abounding love.

It was love that drove me to bound up the mountain and through the brambles to a peak that rounded on a small plateau. Suddenly, there he was! Jaden was standing in a little thicket.

He was among rambling briers. He just looked at me as if to say, "what is all the fuss?" There is absolutely no way to fully explain my feelings at that moment. Relief and joy are not good enough words to explain how I felt. The mountain side may have gotten a hint of my feelings and my emotion as I yelled, "I have found him! I have found him!"

It is as if for a moment the world had stopped. The search was over. The one who was lost has been found. He did not find himself. He was found.

It reminds me of the lost sheep that has gone astray. The shepherd leaves the ninety-nine in search of the one lost sheep. That day the mountain side was not abuzz because of all the children safe at home. It was abuzz because God's created people went out in search of one lost little boy.

I looked at Jaden who was as calm as one can be. He had no idea of the fear that had come into me and his mom. The air had not yet turned cold. It was still daylight, and he could hear the voices of people in the woods.

I could not just reach out and grab Jaden. There was what I call running briers all around him with protruding sharp thorns. I reached in and carefully guided his body around and through the briers. After I got him out, did I scold him? Did I condemn what he had done? I didn't scold or condemn a child who had no concept that he had done something wrong. I held him close and kissed him. I was exuberantly happy and joyful just to have found him. This was a time to celebrate.

That is the way God is when He finds one of his lost children. He celebrates with angels in heaven. When Jesus said that parable of the lost sheep (see Mt. 18:10-14), there was a celebration when the lost sheep was found.

Our creator is a God of life, love, mercy, and forgiveness. His Son, Christ, has shown us the ways of God. Do not let this world, (including teachers and preachers,) fool you. God is love, mercy, forgiveness and more. He is light and life eternal. He is God of heaven and earth; He wants to experience a personal relationship with you. Can you imagine paradise?

The boys, Julia and I seemed to be passing through time at record speed. In the summer, we had a beach vacation at a place with indoor water sports for kids and adults alike. It was a blast for the boys. However, they liked the beach where they often competed for neck rides on G-dad. They liked for me to swing them in circles until they became dizzy. This was not easy since I often became dizzy before they did.

When I think back, I try to visualize how the boys might have experienced this week. I only have my own experience as a child as I try to see through their eyes. Sean (then eight months old) was still seeing his life in the mom's life. Jaden was two plus years old, and Jacques was a little over four years. The older boys were establishing their own identities. These identities would be shaped based upon their life experience.

Jesus says that before one can enter into the kingdom of heaven he must become as a little child (see Mt. 18: 2-4). This same Jesus also told Nicodemus, an educated Pharisee, that he must be born from heaven before he could see God's kingdom. It stands to reason that one must see something before they can enter into it. Therefore, since it is impossible to go back into the mother to be born again, Jesus must be talking about something different.

What does Jesus mean when he says that I must become as a child to enter the kingdom of heaven? Because Jesus is speaking about human impossibilities, where do we find the answer? Since Jesus is the Way, the Truth, and the Life, he must be a pretty good starting place.

Jesus, who is eternal, gave up his position in heaven as God's Son to be borne of a virgin. Humanly speaking, Jesus is a miracle. He was born in the flesh without the aid of man. Jesus was born by the power of God.

Jesus has two different lives. However, they are in unity as one life. God gave us his son. Jesus, gave his life in the flesh in order to live the power of God in the spirit. His identity is both in God and in man. One may ask how this can be possible.

When Jesus said that we must be born again before we can see the kingdom of heaven (see Jn. 3:3). Nicodemus responded. *"How can someone be born, when they are old?"* (Jn. 3:4). The answer lies in the man, Jesus, who existed before and beyond the boundaries of time. Can you imagine being there and looking into the eyes and face of Nicodemus as he tries to understand the words of Jesus?

My friends, we have a beginning which lies outside the boundaries of time. Our beginning is in God Himself who created the earth and all that is in it. Jesus came to take us to a place that is beyond the boundaries of time. By the power of God's Holy Spirit Jesus came to transport us into the kingdom of heaven. Before we can enter into God's kingdom, we must be able to see it. Before we can see it, we must be born again of God.

Remember my boy Jacques, out of the blue, asking me a question one evening saying G-dad "What about sharks?" At first, I did not know what he was talking about, so I did not understand the question. What I failed to understand is that Jacques was listening, at some time in the past, when I was speaking about heaven.

I have spoken more than once about Isaiah 11:6-9. Now another voice was speaking to the mind of Jacques. My friends, the Holy Spirit is active and well. At that moment in time the Holy Spirit was speaking to a little boy. Jacques had at least some part of Isaiah 11:6-9 on his mind. Maybe it was where it says, *"the calf and the lion together and a little child will lead them."*

In this world of conflict and battles for our heart, mind and soul, Jacques had evidently keyed into what we see in the human realm as a story book fantasy. However, when I spoke about this portion of Isaiah, I did not speak of it as a dream or a fantasy because it is heaven's reality. It is not a dream. It is the future of those who know Jesus, who have a personal relationship with him and who are, therefore, known by God through his one and only Son. Our Father in heaven sees us through the Christ in us. We are on a journey becoming like Jesus. Our Father sees us in our completeness, because Jesus is complete.

Can you imagine this little boy trying to reason what dangerous creatures will be like in heaven? "What about a shark, G-dad?" Okay. If a cobra is going to be harmless, and a child can lead a bear, and a wolf will live with a lamb, and a lion will eat straw, what about a shark?

When I realized what Jacques was asking me, I thought about the disciples trying to get Jesus to eat in John chapter four. Jesus told them, *"I have food that you know nothing about."* At that moment Jacques and I in the shower were getting ready to dry, it is appropriate that we were naked as the truth of God was uncovered. It is the naked truth. It is exposed. How wondrously beautiful it is when it is revealed to your heart that a little child can see heaven. I do not know the experiences and challenges that this little boy has experienced. However, during that moment, the Holy Spirit was speaking to his heart, and I thank God that I could comfort him by telling him that in God's heaven nothing will harm him. I told him "Son, you can probably get on that shark's back, hold on to its fin, and go for a ride." I can say these things in total confidence because I believe, and I know, that Jesus was totally sold on the Father's heaven.

There was another time later after Julia and the boys had moved to a home of their own in Athens, Georgia, and Jacques was back for a visit. We were sitting on a swing by the creek. I do not remember what we had been doing that day. This was just relaxing quiet moments of chatting. Jacques suddenly just looked up at me and he asked: "Where is he when I go to Athens?"

My friends, the Holy Spirit is alive and well. I said, "Son, where is who?" He answered, "You know, Jesus!" I would not trade all the painful moments in God's ministry through me if I had to lose this one moment. As a matter of faith, I would not trade the pain and sorrow for earthly treasures. How we deal with the challenges of life reveals who we truly are.

Where is Jesus? How much of our conversation Jacques understood, I do not know. However, I do believe that he heard me when I said, "Son, Jesus goes with you everywhere. Where you are is where Jesus is." That seemed to satisfy Jacques.

The wind of the Spirit was blowing over two of God's created people sitting in a swing. John writes that Jesus replied, *"Very Truly I tell you, no one can see the kingdom of God unless they are born again"* (Jn. 3:3). Matthew writes Jesus said, *"...truly I tell you, unless you change and become like little children, you will never enter the kingdom of heaven"* (Mat. 18:3).

LISTEN FOR THE SPIRIT

Which comes first? When we see the kingdom of heaven, are we born again? If we are born again, then it is imperative that we become like children if we are going to be able to enter into the kingdom of heaven. Jacques believed me, or (better yet) he believed the Spirit of truth that was speaking to his heart.

Religion puts a lot of emphasis on being saved, being born again, and accepting Jesus. Religions have membership requirements. They often have lofty phrases and pronouncements that come from the bible. We go through these rituals, and it is supposed that we are a born-again Christian. I dare say that these rituals are not worth a nickel unless you are truly born from above. Then you must become like a child. The Holy Spirit will not take you faster than you can or are willing to absorb and know.

Transcending the flesh to live in the realm of eternity cannot be accomplished by human means or effort. When John the apostle says "*born of God*" that is exactly what John means. When Jesus says in Matthew 18:4 that you must become like a child, that is what Jesus means.

There are no human ways into the kingdom of heaven. There are no short cuts into God's kingdom. Jesus is the way into God's kingdom. Jesus reveals the truth about God's kingdom, and it is in his life that we see God's eternal kingdom.

There is a section in the Methodist service where the congregation is reciting together some of the church ritual. This section is a truth. However, I have often wondered how many people really understood this truth. I believe that the only words that matter as they relate to God are the words that flow from your heart. The words that I am speaking about are the words where the congregation recites from the hymnal. These words are, "You are forgiven." Are you really forgiven just by repeating these words?

Yes, you are forgiven whether you repeat these words or not. The accuser has been condemned and you are forgiven. On the cross, we can see the heart of God in Jesus. In His teaching on the cross Jesus asked the Father to forgive the offenders of God. He asked for forgiveness for those who hated him. He asked for forgiveness for those who betrayed him. He asked forgiveness for those who beat him, spit on him, crowned him with thorns and mocked him. Jesus asked for all humanity to be forgiven. Jesus was paying the price for the redemption of all people. "You are forgiven." However, the question is; have you received God's forgiveness? Have you received Jesus? Do you believe in Jesus?

The apostle John writes in chapter one of his gospel, it is those who receive Jesus and believe in him, who are given the right and the power to become God's child.

It is one thing for someone to offer you a place in their life. It is another thing when you accept that offer. Until the offer is accepted, it is like a gift that remains unopened. Until you open the gift, it is of no value to you. If you do not open and receive a gift, you have no idea of the treasures that lie within the gift.

"You are forgiven." Jesus asked the Father for you to be forgiven. In doing so. He committed his life to pay the cost for you. The price has been paid. Now the Spirit of truth is wooing God's children back into a relationship with God. Through Jesus, you are offered a right standing with God so you can begin to live life in the confidence of an eternal child of God.

My friends, God is more than rituals and reciting. Yet these do have a place. At Bogart United Methodist Church in Georgia, we had a lady who began the opening for Sunday school.

She always began with, "This is the day that the Lord has made. Let us rejoice and be glad in it." That is a beautiful acclamation which we all should begin each day of our life with and mean it.

You might say that there are times in life when it is not a joyful day. Why would anyone want to rejoice in the midst of some of the tragedies of life? I believe that when you know Jesus, you have the right and the power to rejoice and be thankful in all things, even though it can be difficult.

Jesus told his disciples that they would be betrayed and that some of them would be put to death (see Lu. 21:16). Then he told them in 21:18, that "...*not a hair of your head will perish.*" These verses represent your two different lives. One life is in the flesh. Regardless of what happens or what we do, this flesh will die. In verse 18, Jesus is talking about your eternal spiritual being, your soul. This is your life in God and God in you. This life will never perish.

The place that Jesus is leading his followers is to a place in Christ, and him in you. In this place you begin to live in the realm of eternity. That is a place before time and beyond time. When your life begins to focus outside the limits of time, you can begin to be glad and rejoice in all things. Nothing can harm the God in you and you in God. When your life begins to focus outside the limits of time, you can begin to be glad and rejoice in all things. Nothing can harm the God in you and you in God, even though you are now residing in this temporal body of flesh. One day you will begin to live the eternal day. Listen to John as he writes in Revelation 22:5,

"There will be no more night. They will not need the light of a lamp or the light of the sun, for the Lord God will give them light. And they will reign forever and forever".

Forever is forever. We are all challenged to begin living in God this very hour. When you accept God's forgiveness, your eyes will begin to open and you will begin to see the kingdom on earth as it is in heaven.

How I long for all my children (This includes grandchildren and, of course, all children) to know God and be known by God. This is absolutely the greatest gift known to humanity. However, it is better to not have the gift if it has been bastardized. What I mean by this is that too often humankind has sought to improve the gift by adding their own doctrinal touch to the bible.

Many people know the doctrines of their religion better than they know the Bible. The saddest thing is that they often interpret the bible based upon their doctrines which often change a little bit here and a little bit there. Can this be sound doctrine? Are the scriptures not enough? What about the books outside the cannon? Could they not have been inspired of God?

There are many questions about religion and spiritual life. Religion itself has many faces. However, the individual spirit life is another matter. There are deceiving spirits, spirits of discouragement, fear, anxiety, depression, and many more. The apostle Paul says that we, meaning those who follow Christ, are not against flesh and blood, but that we battle with forces of evil in the heavenly realm (Eph. 6:12).

So, what is a spiritual life? For the Christian, it is a life that listens to and follows the Spirit of truth. I want my boys to follow the Spirit of truth which Jesus promised. The reality is that this Spirit is here now. This Spirit condemns Satan and the spiritual forces of evil. When I spoke with Jacques about the Paradise of God, he believed me. However, Jacques did not believe me only. For Jacques to go as deeply into thought as he did concerning Isaiah 11:6-9, he needed help. He had to be thinking about this beautiful Paradise of God. As he attempted to rationalize this, I believe that the spiritual forces of evil put doubt and questions into his mind. I could see the spirits of fear and doubt at work in Jacques' mind as he envisioned sharks and other animals. The Spirit of truth came to the rescue of this little boy. Ask G-dad! He will tell you about a shark in God's paradise. The same thing was true when Jacques asked me where Jesus was when he went to Athens. The Spirit of truth came to the rescue. When I said, "Son, he is with you wherever you are", he seemed at ease and satisfied. For my grandson, Jacques, I pray that the Spirit of truth will continue in the battle against spiritual forces of evil that seek to destroy my boy.

One evening me and the three boys were sitting at the table. It was Monday. The boys were with me when we at God's Dwelling Place had our services at the United Community Bank building. The message that day was about the real and true born-of-God personal relationship with Jesus. As our relationship with Jesus grows, we begin to see the revelation of the Spirit of truth in our lives, and in the life of others. We, too often, being unaware or unreceptive to the reality of the Spirit, do not recognize when the Spirit of truth is intervening in our lives and in the lives of those around us. This can be especially true when it comes to children.

Living in God's realm is when we can go beyond this temporary life and live beyond concepts and ideas of humanity. We begin to live in the eternal realm of God. When any person moves into this realm and begins to live God's reality, they have a new zest for life. Their ability to live in the present is enhanced. The past is reflective history, and our tomorrows cannot be used until they become today.

Now, back to me and my boys sitting around the table. Sean was in a highchair. The food was on the plates. As usual, we said our prayer that always seemed to end with "Amen, Hallelujah!" The boys had gotten into this kind of emphasis at the end of our prayers. I cannot remember how the discussion got to Jesus but somehow it did. The helper Jesus promised was at work.

At our Sunday service we had a message about the realness of God's presence. While we were eating, the Holy Spirit posed a question to me. "Do the boys know where Jesus is right now?" So, I asked them, "Where is

Jesus right now?" I can still see Jacques as he quickly rises out of his chair, and he points to a vacant chair. I say vacant. I do not know what Jacques saw. However, he emphatically spoke with boldness. His voice rang with a heartfelt truth. He said Jesus is right there in that chair.

On Sunday, I had suddenly found myself pointing to what appeared to be a vacant chair. I said Jesus should be so real to you that you can feel his presence as if he were sitting right there in that chair. What Jacques saw at that time I do not know. However, I do believe that the Holy Spirit was revealing truth when Jacques pointed to the chair. For these words to come from the mouth of a child reminds me that faith is born in us when we begin the journey of our spiritual life. It is when we become like a child that we can enter into the kingdom of heaven.

When you are born new, then you can see the kingdom of heaven. When you become like a child, you can enter into the kingdom of heaven. There is a huge problem in portions of our religious communities. The problem is that many people actually believe that they can accomplish salvation for themselves and others. This is probably true of actions more than words. When we become desperate to get others saved, we can easily get in front of the Holy Spirit.

Many religions have this formula. Get them to the altar. Recite a prayer or what is called the sinners' prayer. Make a confession and then suddenly through these rituals you are confirmed as born again. In essence, you have got yourself saved because you have met all of the human requirements. What about the personal relationship as a child of God? If I haven't missed something, the apostle John says that God's children are born of God (see Jn. 1:13).

Since God's children are born of God, why should we become so wrapped up in doing something that only God can do? If we truly follow the example of Jesus, we discover that our focus should be to allow God to do his work through a vessel of flesh that completely yields to God's will. Since we can do nothing apart from God, our focus must be to allow God to accomplish his purpose through us. The good news is not about humankind accomplishing something. It is allowing what has already been accomplished in us to manifest itself.

When Jacques said that Jesus is right there in that chair, I am tempted to take credit for his words because he heard them from me. Yet, it was not from me alone. It was from the manifestation of God's Spirit working through me.

Did Jesus tell the disciples in John 9:2 that the work of the blind man would be revealed? That is, did Jesus say this man had listened and become very smart, and he would make naked these religious imposters? No! What Jesus said is that the work of God in the blind man will be revealed (Jn. 9:3).

My boy Jacques' affirmations to me reveal more than any altar call can ever accomplish. Most altar calls come with a certain amount of pressure from the speaker. Whether intended or not, it becomes a display of more about the person than God. People will travel a long way to go to healing ministries as if some person claims to have influence over the ability of God to heal.

My grandson confirms for me the greatest healing known to humankind. It is the healing that takes place in one's life when they know within their heart, mind and spirit that God lives in them, and takes them into himself: Then they begin to share the life of the eternal Christ. This is not some fairytale. This is God's reality. His children become his forever. Even though these bodies of flesh will die, God's eternal children will never die. God will supply that new eternal spiritual body. One day we will be like the eternal man who is Christ; And, yes, we will eat food. Jesus ate in front of the disciples after his resurrection.

SIX

CLOUDY DAYS COMING

I t was Julia's birthday (August 22). She was thirty-four years old. She had worked hard in school and had accepted the challenge of raising three boys as a single mom. She is a beautiful woman. However, she has been challenged emotionally for many years. I became aware of her challenges during her teen years.

She is smart and she is my beautiful daughter. Experimenting with drugs began early in her life. She was a great gymnast. However, after a skiing injury sidelined her for a little while she began to experiment with drugs. I will just say at times she was a challenging young girl fast becoming a woman.

When she called me about picking up the boys, I believe that she was comforted knowing that they would be ok with me. She had been a good mom and she loved her boys. I believe getting the boys freed her up to celebrate. The problem was that this day led Julia back into an out-of-control life. The boy's dad and I would have to take charge. Try as I might I could not rescue my beautiful daughter at the time. I wanted to help her, but with the drugs it became impossible. I had to direct my attention to these three boys. It would take a long time, but eventually my daughter would come to her senses. In the meantime, it became me, my boys and God.

I can only imagine what the boys were feeling when their mom was suddenly gone. I remember that afternoon when the daycare called and said Julia had not picked up the boys. A short time later Julia called and said that she was stuck in traffic, and would I pick up the boys? Of course! We are a family.

One could say that the boys were mine and of my own blood because I was their mother's dad. Yet, that would only be a very narrow view of our relationship. Sure, part of their being originated in me as well as a long list of other people. If we go back far enough, it is plain to me that their true source of life comes from the creator of all things. However, for now let's just say, as we became a family, a miracle was taking place.

Jesus talks about this miracle of relationships throughout his ministry as we know it on earth. He often referred to himself as one with the Father. He would say such crazy things like *"I am in the Father and the Father is in me."* He told his disciples that they had seen the Father because they had seen him.

ETERNAL LOVE

What was taking place between me, Jacques, Jaden and Sean was a miracle of a deep-rooted relationship. We may try to plan for the future, but relationships are not planned. They are truly born. When they are born out of love, they are absolutely beautiful beyond expression. How can I describe a love that overpowers your heart, a love that melts your heart, mind and soul?

I have prayed to know Jesus more intimately, more personally and more passionately. I never knew how much pain I would undergo because of love. I never knew how much of the beauty of God I would discover, until I gave my heart away to the innocent.

Life for my boys was like a ship adrift. These innocent hearts did not know where they would land, as they were tossed to and fro, on the sea of life. For them life was normal, but these innocent hearts have an inner desire for a life where they can feel safe and at home.

Humankind has gone adrift on the sea of life, exercising their free will to choose the direction of their lives. What direction will they choose? Will they choose to be led by the one who created them or by the deceiver? There is no middle road.

My boys have melted my heart. I see the back and forth of a split family. I see little hearts that are pulled. I also see the heart of God as the boys melted my heart. It is in this place that I know that I melted the heart of my Father in heaven.

I know more deeply the heart of God as God yearns for all of his children to know just how much their Father in heaven loves them. He wants you to know that you are deeply loved with a love more powerful than death itself. So powerful that the God of life sent his Son to prove to humanity that his love is more powerful than death.

God has a desperate love for each human heart. Even now God is pouring out this eternal love for all who are willing to receive it. God himself is the teacher, he is the truth. Jesus shows us the way into the heart of God and his eternal kingdom that will never end.

In his life Jesus teaches love. His life is a virtual love story. It is incredible what God has done through this one man. Jesus' life reveals God's love for all humanity. From beginning to end (and there truly is no end) Jesus pours out God's love over the earth. He is like an unstoppable river. It flows and it flows. You can try to damn it up, but it will escape. It is a raging fire in the heart of God. It is unstoppable. It is without measure. You can give it away, and the more you give, the more you receive. I could say that it is amazing, but how do you describe amazing? I have prayed to know Jesus intimately, and my Father in heaven is obliging.

Let me make it clear. I love all my children and all of my grandchildren dearly. It is just that in this stage of my life, I have found myself more intimately involved with these boys. Relationships happen. However, they build based upon the investment of time, energy and attitude.

When I had Sean by myself, we became a twosome. That was just life. Being thrust into the role of both a mom and a dad provided an encounter of which I had never dreamed. It has brought me into a greater depth of understanding of the phenomenal love of God. God taught me in such a way that I could feel his joy, his pain, his delight and his suffering, as I began to feel first-hand God's deep affection for me.

KISSED BY GOD

One night when Sean was a little over a year old, we were lying in bed. The day was done. The shower and playing were over. I do not remember why, but my heart and soul were troubled. Emotionally, I was sinking. Lying there on my back, the devil's demons were seeking to drag me into the pit of self-pity.

Suddenly, without warning, the most amazing thing happened. Only God knew what it would take to defeat this evil seeking to rob me of life this night. My defender, the Spirit of Truth, was on guard. A prayer would be answered. In my despair, the spiritual forces of evil had invaded God's territory. **I am his territory**. I am a dwelling place for the Father and the Son. God's love would overpower these forces of evil with a simple kiss from the heart of God. Without warning, the infant Sean lying by my side leaned over and kissed me. It was not Sean alone who kissed me. Just as God worked in the blind man, he worked through an infant. I will never forget the night that God leaned over and kissed the cheek of one of his own. God kissed me. Yes, he did, God truly kissed me.

As I begin to know Christ more personally and more intimately, it has become apparent to me that the student was ready for the teacher to appear. I did not know that the stage was set. The characters were chosen. The stars of the drama which would begin to unfold were a ten-month old, a two and a half-year old, and a five-year old boy.

The leading man was the ten-month old. The real star of the drama operated behind the scenes. The divine character who will direct this drama thereby bringing me more deeply into the relationship for which I had prayed.

Having one's heart more deeply penetrated by love brings with it great longings, sufferings, and pain. It is not like human pain or suffering. It is heart pain and suffering that comes from a longing from deep within one's soul for life to be made right. It is a longing for peace, for love, for joy, and for the hearts of compassion to prevail. It is a longing for the heart of a child to be at peace and to know without any doubt they are truly loved, with a love that even death cannot destroy.

It is impossible for the human mind to fully grasp a love more powerful than death. We know who the star is behind the scenes. The main player in any drama for a disciple of Christ is the Spirit of truth, the Holy Spirit.

KNOWING THE SPIRIT OF TRUTH

When you begin to seek, hear, and listen to the voice of God, it is because the Spirit of truth is at work. This is the Advocate which Jesus promised you and me.

There are other spirits that function in and around us. When we have received Jesus into ourselves, we allow him to take us into the dimension where God reigns. We still must deal with the spiritual forces of evil. I say this to remind myself that I am on a journey where the destination is the heart of God. As a disciple of Jesus, it is the place from which my life and the life of all disciples must function.

If we are to live our lives from where God lives, we must be guided by the Spirit of truth. That is why I pray earnestly for guidance by the Spirit of truth. I am promised by "The Christ" that when I pray in his name, my prayers will be answered.

With that said, how then do I pray in the name of Jesus? I must pray as Jesus would pray. How is that? As we look at the life of Jesus, we can see how he lived, how he prayed, in the will and purpose of God. He prayed, *"Father not my will but your will."* Jesus gave his life. That is, he gave all of his life for the purpose of God. So, we too must give our life for the purpose and will of God. When we do this, we pray accordingly.

One might say that there is no way to know how they can give their whole life away. Before the Spirit of truth can guide us, we must have first given the Spirit a place in our life. To do this, we must undergo a life exchange.

In this exchange, we give up the life that leads to death, for the life that transforms us into the eternal child of God. Jesus says that the flesh counts for nothing, that his words are spirit and life. When we look at the exchange, what we should see is our dying flesh being freely given in exchange for the glorious body of Christ. When we go through this exchange, we too will become not only capable but willing participants in the eternal life of Christ.

I know that it takes a tremendous amount of faith to truly say, "Father, thy will and not mine," and mean it. We all struggle with giving up control of our life choices. God has given us a free will and we want to use it. In this one case, we can have our cake and eat it too. Our Father in heaven will not violate our freedom to choose our direction in life.

Our Father is offering us a guide which is the Spirit of truth. The Spirit is just that – "a guide." This guide will always lead us in the direction of truth. There are other spirits that will cunningly try to deceive us and lie to us. They will lead us down the path that leads to death. God's Spirit will always guide us to truth.

We all have a choice. We can be guided by the spirit that deceives us, lies to us, and leads us into the darkness of death, or we can allow the Spirit of truth to lead us into the light of eternal life. It will always be our choice. As for me, I choose truth, light, and life.

When we come to realize that we are God's eternal child, and he loves us more than life; only then can we truly begin to pray in the Spirit of Jesus. When we pray in his spirit, we are praying for truth, light, and life. Jesus has demonstrated that God loves us with all of his strength, all of his heart, all of his mind, and all of his soul.

As the drama with my boys begins to unfold, my Father in heaven is committed to me. He guides me by this Spirit of truth, and I pray for this spirit to always win over those deceiving spirits.

THE SEA OF WAVES

Life again is going to change. Like a ship on the ocean in a violent wind, the direction of my life would make a dramatic change. At the time I had no idea of the challenges or the lessons to be learned. I had no idea just how much my ability to love would be enhanced. I did not know just how much I would come to know more deeply God's passionate love for all humanity. I did not know how desperately I needed the Spirit of truth to guide my life in so many ways.

I prayed for guidance at every step. I was still pastor of a small church. I had begun to see a woman again. Before Julia and the boys came, I had dated a woman for a couple of years. However, this relationship had ended months ago. This was an interesting time in a single person's life. I believe it was prayer and the work of the Holy Spirit that brought me through these stages of life.

God honors sincere prayers; those prayers which ask for God's will and purpose. One cannot be a disciple of Jesus or an apostle unless they are sincere about seeking the will and purpose of God for their life. What you must realize when you say that you follow Jesus is that you are following the wisest, most powerful man who ever walked the earth. To follow Jesus, the Spirit of truth must guide you.

This Spirit of truth reveals what he has seen and heard from the Father and the Son. The nature of wind, which you cannot control, is this Spirit. I do know and believe that it is from God. However, I am totally in awe of how this Spirit manifests itself, even though, mankind often seeks to control and manipulate that which is out of their control.

In a sermon one day, a spontaneous thought entered my mind. I was talking about the real and sincere presence of God at all times. Even when you are in the bathroom. I don't like to think about it, but he is there too. My grandson Jacques was present during this sermon.

If someone were to secretly follow me around, they would often think that I was apologizing to myself when I say, "excuse me", or "I am sorry", or "forgive me". Keep in mind, humanly speaking, I am alone. However, I have become more and more conscious that I am never alone.

I can understand why Paul says that he is constantly in prayer or in discussion with God. What a child of God must come to terms with is that Jesus will never turn his face from us. We may look away, but he never looks away. Realizing this one night as I was reading out loud, I became breathless and unable to speak. I could not speak for a moment because the Spirit of truth had just revealed to me that in my darkest hours when I questioned, doubted and denied the existence of God; I had turned as completely as humanly possible from God. I had denied his existence, but he has never denied me. Even in my confusion about God, and in my pain, God would never reveal himself in a way that was not true to his nature. I was looking for the God that I had received from people of the flesh, but this god is impossible to find.

How could you identify with an entity that is completely beyond anything that you can humanly comprehend? If God is Spirit, then you will only come to know him in the Spirit. This is not your spirit. It is God's Spirit that is given to you when you are born again. With your spiritual birth, comes the power that can transform you into God's blessed child. This is a phenomenal transformation. You are literally transformed from a doomed mortal being into eternal life.

Understanding Jesus and his teaching is dependent on the work of God's Holy Spirit of which you have given a home. This Spirit lives in you. Your body is now his temple. This spirit will begin to reveal God's truths to you and your reborn life will be guided by the power of your creator.

When my Father in heaven led me to Jesus, I began to learn the truth about God. Jesus became my teacher aided by the Spirit of truth.

Getting back to the sermon when Jacques was present! Without a thought, I suddenly found myself pointing to an empty chair (I know this is a repeat, but it fits into the story). The wind of the spirit flowed through me with no effort and no thought on my part. I must say I am humanly and spiritually in agreement with the words that came forth. I do not believe that the Spirit will give me words that I do not embrace in my spirit and in my heart. I also believe that the Spirit of truth will protect me from the wrong and evil thoughts that come into my mind.

We must remember that the words spoken to Adam and Eve in the garden were evil disguised as words of enlightenment when they were enticed to be disobedient to God (see Gen. 3:1-4).

Like a violent wind the words that came forth were simple words for those who seek to follow Jesus. As I pointed to the vacant chair, the words simply flowed forth. They were real. They were simple, and they were truth. They are just as true this hour as they were then. They serve to remind us that Jesus is real and that his presence is in every part of the Christ-like life. Jesus, (for the Christian), must be as real as if he were sitting right there in that chair. The Spirit was not finished with this message.

A day or two later I was sitting at the table with my boys Sean, Jaden and Jacques. Dinner was prepared and we were ready to eat. We had said our prayer which ended with "Amen" and a resounding "Hallelujah!" I do not remember what stage of dinner we were in, and I do not remember how the discussion of Jesus began. However, for whatever reason, it was impressed upon me to ask, "Where is Jesus right now?" Jacques rose from his seat with a broad smile on his face as he excitedly pointed to an empty chair speaking with confidence and excitement in his voice and said, "He is right there in that chair." I was blessed at that meal by a young boy and the wind of the Spirit (Jn. 3:8). My friends, the Holy Spirit is alive and well.

When Jesus was speaking with Nicodemus about being born again before you can have the ability to see the kingdom of heaven, Nicodemus was completely confused. He was a knowledgeable Pharisee, but for him the words Jesus spoke were about an impossible task. Jesus words were truthful, and they spoke about a transition of life that was attainable in spirit.

However, Jesus' declaration was not attainable humanly speaking. Being born again is not the result of rituals or altar calls, or fear of hell. Fear is not any part of who God is, but still it is used for persuasion. We cannot persuade anyone to become a Christian. It is the Spirit that does the persuading through those who allow God's work to be done, because they believe (see Jn. 6:28,29).

Humanity, in great wisdom, often begins to think that they can do God's work. When I say great wisdom, I mean great human wisdom. In Jesus' day the religious leaders had it all together from their own perspective. They had God where they wanted God. They seemed to believe they were in control of the way to God with their laws, their rules and their traditions.

Jesus warned the religious leaders of his day, but they could not hear him. Jesus even tells them why they cannot hear him. He tells them that their actions reveal that they are children of the devil. Jesus did not call them children of the devil to hurt them (see Jn. 8:44). This was an honest warning to let them know the spirit of death and lies that were leading them. He wanted them to know they were not doing their duty; they were leading people astray.

It is very easy to go with your own spirit or with the wrong spirit when you think that you can use a child's moment of revelation to further your ministry. Do you see and understand the words I just used? "Your ministry" or my ministry! A true ministry is not a ministry of human origin. A true ministry is God's ministry. Humanly speaking, you or I can do nothing to further the ministry of God. God's ministry consists of eternal work that can only be accomplished by eternal hands.

Jesus told his disciples, (and he tells us today,) that we can do **nothing** apart from him. However, if we abide in him and he is in us, nothing is impossible. I believe that Nicodemus who came to Jesus at night eventually came to understand how he can be born again (see Jn. 3:4). Nicodemus became ritually unclean when he helped bury Jesus. He also risked his reputation and position as a Pharisee.

Nicodemus did the right thing when he questioned the words of Jesus. It is the right thing for us today to have a discussion with God as we struggle to gain insight. God will not deprive a sincere heart of the light of truth. When we find ourselves in a dark place in life, it is okay to say, "My God, my God, why have you forsaken me?" If indeed, you feel forsaken. He is your Abba, (Daddy,) and he will never turn his face from you.

Recalling Jacques' question about sharks, I sincerely believe that the Holy Spirit, (Spirit of Truth,) was at work in Jacques deflecting the arrows of death from Satan as Jacques pondered on the words of Isaiah chapter 11. Can you imagine the enemy's attack on the spirit of this small child as he tried to envision a world of total peace? Knowing the dangerous and challenging aspects of life, Satan would rather Jacques see God's paradise as just another fairy tale.

As we run to and fro in life, we are busy, busy, busy. Our minds are racing. There is always something to accomplish or distractions to occupy our minds. We want to escape. Yes, we want to escape! Instead of hearing God's voice, we choose to be constantly bombarded by other distractions. If we just listen, we will hear God speak even in the hustle and bustle of life. He is speaking. Are you listening?

One day, I found myself on a swing by our fire pit next to a small stream. Jacques was at my side. He and I talk about a lot of things. A lot of times it is reprimands because of his actions. He is a beautiful boy, but his life has had its complications. Most reprimands are because of his treatment of his younger brothers. He can be beautiful with them, or he can be a real pain in the rear.

This day we were just sitting. The swing was moving ever so slightly. You could hear the cascade of the stream. The weather was mild. It was quiet. However, I believe that a visitor was present. Again, Jacques came out with half a question. What about when I go to Athens to visit my Dad? What about Jesus? Where is he when I am in Athens? Out of the mouth of babes comes wisdom.

The wisdom is to recognize how even a small child can feel the difference in a place where the spirit is welcome and sought. I do not know why Jacques would ask this question unless the Holy Spirit was at work in his heart. In this day and age, it is not too normal for a six-year-old to ask questions about an eternal God of peace and love. The Spirit of Truth wanted this little innocent child to know that his God was always with him. I told Jacques that Jesus was always with him. I said Jesus goes wherever you go.

My heart yearns for this boy to be taught the truth about the one true God whose identity we can see in the life of Jesus. Jesus knew that even death of his body was only a small part of his existence (see Jn. 6:63).

One might ask, "How can death be life?" Jesus told us that he was in charge of his life. Jesus told us that he would lay his life down and that he would take it up again. Jesus said that no one takes his life, but that he gives his life. John 3:16 says that God gave his Son. The Father completely gave us his Son.

Who lays down the physical life of Jesus? The Spirit of Jesus lays his life down. Who takes up the physical life of Jesus? The spiritual Jesus who has no interruption of life takes up this life that he laid down.

Jesus says that the flesh is nothing, but that the Spirit is full of life (see Jn. 6:63). Death is not life. Jesus, in fulfilling the purpose of God, yielded his life to the will of God. Jesus knows that there is a greater life than our dying bodies of flesh. He wants his followers to know this and believe this from the depth of their heart, mind and soul. Jesus shows us the way to life as he passes through death without any interruption of his spiritual journey.

Followers of Jesus are promised that one day we will "*bear the image of the heavenly man*" (1 Cor. 15:49). When I read John 20:17, I see here a transition even for the body of Jesus. Jesus says to Mary Magdalene, "*Do not hold on to me, for I have not yet ascended to the Father.*" Later on, greeting

Thomas and the other disciples, Jesus would invite Thomas to touch him. I believe that at this point Jesus had ascended to the Father and was back again in the body to complete his assignments before final departure.

KNOWN BY GOD

Matthew, Mark and Luke give us a picture of Moses and Elijah, alive on the mountain of transfiguration (see Mat. 17:3 & Mk. 9:4). This brings truth to Jesus' statement to Martha where Jesus tells her that those who believe will never die (see Jn. 11:26). It is imperative that those who attest to being followers of Jesus are truly born of God. You cannot breathe out the eternal spirit unless you have first breathed it in.

When I pray for the gift of God to be bestowed upon Jacques, I believe that God will honor this prayer as far as it is in alignment with God to accomplish God's purpose. For me, the miracle of God working in a child is a beautiful revelation to my heart. I cannot always be with my children. However, my prayer is that they will know the one true God, and better yet, as Paul says, to be known by God.

Paul says that it is better to be known by God than to know God (1Cor. 8:3, Gal. 4:9). I have often pondered just what he means. This is where I am today. Paul believes that Jesus is the one and only Son of God. God's many children are born as a result of the redeeming power that is in Christ; therefore, God knows his children as they are in Christ, and he is in them. He does not know you as the fallen Adam. He knows you by the Spirit of the resurrected Christ that is in you. It is your minute by minute, hour by hour, and day by day relationship that reveals whether you truly know God and are known by God.

The apostle Paul gives us a qualifier when it comes to being known by God. Paul writes in 1 Corinthians 8:3; "*But whoever loves God is known by God.*" It is loving that best describes the character of God. God knows you love him when you love him with the kind of obedient love modeled by Jesus. When you love him, you receive God's heart, and he gives you, his heart. Then you become known by God as his child.

To know Christ is to suffer and die with him. When you receive Christ into your life, you begin to die to self, to experience the resurrected power of Jesus in, over, above and under your life. You begin to live the resurrected life. You no longer live in the dust of the flesh. You now live by the power of the eternal Spirit of Christ, and your Father knows you in your completeness because Christ in you is complete. Through Christ you have become God's eternal child.

I am the oldest of eight children. When I married Julia's mom Lorraine, she had three children. So, with three boys, I was not totally out of my comfort zone. However, this time I was alone. I was dating, but the twenty-four/seven for the boys was on my shoulders.

A MEMORABLE SCHOOL DAY

Jacques was five and ready to start to school. The situation caught their dad Reico off guard, and he needed some time to make arrangements for the boys. At the same time, he would begin to get things in order for Jacques to start to school in Athens, Georgia.

In the meantime, I followed through with arrangements for Jacques to begin school in Hayesville, North Carolina. I will never forget taking Jacques to school that first day. We had gotten up early for breakfast. I dropped Jaden and Sean off at Elf daycare. Then it was just me and Jacques.

I can still picture taking Jacques into his classroom to meet his teachers. He was excited, apprehensive and smiling. I think that it was a nervous and excited smile. What was the young boy feeling? Who can possibly know? No man or woman can know what is going on in the heart and mind of a little boy. We can have feelings for a child's situation. Even these feelings are often determined by our own personal experience of life.

That is where this little boy was. His experiences in life were creating within himself varying degrees of comfort and discomfort. However, Jacques had had a very positive experience at the Elf daycare.

I believe that his experience at Elf was a building block to help him move through the ever-changing stages of life. I left Jacques that day a little nervous, but content as he looked forward to the next step in his journey of life.

SEVEN

CREATED IN GOD'S IMAGE

lot had happened since I wrote my letter to God. I was looking for companionship and passion in my life. I would never have dreamed that my Father in heaven would take me on the journey in life that I found myself immersed in.

I was alone and I had three boys. A ten-month old! A four year and three-month old and a two year and five-month-old. I was sixty-seven years old. The situation was completely out of the hemisphere. This was not normal. However, my Father saw this situation as a great opportunity to teach me about Himself.

At the time, I had no idea of what God was doing to enlighten me about his true nature. I became a mother and a father to these boys. In a sense I was their center. I did not realize it at the time, but my Father, knowing the future, had brought us together. The student was ready, and the teacher appeared. God, the ultimate teacher, was the director of this drama.

I did not know it at the time, but the Holy Spirit, which is the Spirit of truth, was the main player. The Father knew my heart and he knew that my desire was for a passionate love affair. My flesh had one idea about what this affair looked like, and my internal spirit had a different idea.

My Father had looked into my heart and saw the passion for true love and truth that he had planted there. When God created human beings and breathed life into them, the life that he breathed was his life. My father had planted the image of himself into me.

If I am created in the image of God, this image is much more than flesh and blood. This image bears the character of God himself, and Jesus tells us that God is spirit. I believe that I am created in the image of God and, therefore, I have the seed of God within me.

Although God's heart and God's nature has been planted in me, I also suffer the desire of the flesh to be its own god. It was in disobedience that Adam and Eve chose their will over God's will when they succumbed to temptation in the garden. At this point, all humanity entered into a war between the flesh and the spirit. My Father's desire is to bring humanity back to the place where we can fulfill our purpose and destiny. For those who can believe it, God has corrected that fall into fear, darkness and death. We can rise again to a place where there is no death.

A great teacher has come and shown us the way into our Father's eternal truth. Some would rise up in arms if I said that Jesus never died. However, it is clear to me that there are two distinct parts to the life of Jesus. His Father is God. Mary became pregnant through the power of the Holy Spirit. She gave birth to a baby of flesh and blood. At his baptism the spirit descended on him.

Luke writes, "*the Holy Spirit descended on him in bodily form like a dove*" (Lu. 3:22). In Luke 4:1 it says that "*Jesus, full of the Holy Spirit, left the Jordan and was led by the spirit into the wilderness.*"

All of Jesus was led into the wilderness. What I mean is that the flesh and blood Jesus, along with the spiritual Jesus, was led into the wilderness. It is Jesus' spiritual power that controls the flesh. Jesus was always in control of his total being. Jesus has shown us how we too. can be in control of our total being. It is not that the flesh is bad, and the spirit is good. All of God's creation is good. However, when we look at the world, we see the tragedy of a humanity seeking to be their own god. We see a humanity that says my will not God's will.

Jesus, with his total life, shows us the way into life eternal. Jesus laid his temporary life down. His flesh and blood suffered death. He told his disciples that some of them would be put to death (Lu. 21:16). Then he tells them not a hair of their head would be harmed (Lu. 21:18).

What do you really mean, Jesus? Death! No harm! Jesus means both. Anyway we look at it, this covering of flesh and blood is going to die. We know this. Jesus is pointing the way to who you can become by the power of God. He shows us the defeat of death and the way into the Father's dimension.

The Son of Man laid his life down and the eternal man took his life up again. Jesus now invites his followers to do the same thing. What Jesus is asking us to do is trade this temporary life for eternal life. What this means is that you are going to allow God to guide your temporary life, which is a small part, a very tiny part of your eternal life. Do not worry, your Father will never violate your free will to choose your direction in life.

What is happening when you die with Jesus is that you are also going to be raised with him to never die. At Lazarus' grave Jesus told his friend Martha that *"whoever lives by believing in me will never die"* (Jn. 11:26a). The key here are the words whoever lives by believing in Jesus. Scripture says that even the demons believe. If we look closely at what John wrote, it is living by believing. This is where we go beyond believing that Jesus exists to living his life. This is more than a sinner's prayer. It is an implementation of the life of Jesus in you and you in him.

Humanly speaking it is impossible to live the life of Jesus apart from Jesus. You cannot accomplish eternal things in the flesh which chooses its own will. In baptism, you symbolically die as you are submerged (or sprinkled). You are dying to the old self in order that you may rise to the new self. This is symbolic of what must take place at a deeper level. At the deeper level is where you follow Jesus as your heart becomes aligned for the purpose and will of God.

Giving your heart to Christ is not a controlling religion. It is freeing you from the passions of life to live your destiny as a child of God. Without God neither you nor I can experience the most passionate love affair of our lives. Our Father will pour his love into our hearts, and it will overflow into the life of our spouse, our family, our friends, those we meet, and yes even to our enemies. The passion of my Father is the most powerful thing on earth and in heaven.

Yes, the flesh and blood Jesus died a cruel death. However, the God of heaven and earth put life back into that body and Jesus, the one and only Son of God, took that life back up again. As we begin to live the resurrected life of Jesus, we will begin to see that we are becoming the image of God.

At this very moment in time. my heart is flooded in love. It aches for my boys. I can see the tossing to and fro of their lives. It. is not that they are in a bad situation, humanly speaking, but I know them. I have been touched by them. At this moment in time, you might say that they are the apple of my eye. Why, now at seventy-two years old, am I so concerned about three boys? Through these boys it has dawned on me that I am the apple of my Father's eye.

Just as I am desperate for my boys, my Father is desperate for me. I believe that God is complete and does not need anyone to do anything for him. However, in the life of Christ, we see a Father who is passionately and desperately in love with all of his created people.

It is through these boys that God has revealed to me how much he loves me. He has revealed to me my new heart. It is his very own heart that I have allowed to come into my life and reveal the love potential planted within me. It is so vast that when I try to picture it, it expands into the universe to places unknown. It is so big that it is beyond my ability to fathom how high, how wide, how deep, (Eph 3:20)

As my mind soars the universe to travel beyond the stars, I wonder if there is a place beyond the stars. What is this touch of the spirit that I cannot grasp? What is this love that is pouring out, even this hour, from heaven above? It is beyond my comprehension, yet I can bathe in it. It covers my body. It enters my mouth. I take it in, but I am never full. It creates a hunger that will not go away. I eat it. I drink it, but I am never full. What is it? What is this feeling? It flows through every pore of my body. I give it away and more and more flows in. I could explode in my desire to give it away. What is it that I am receiving as I am compelled to give? It is the indescribable love of God. What has brought me to this place of neediness? Three small boys and the spirit of the eternal living God. Jesus was a mad man according to the Pharisees. Perhaps, from the human perspective, Jesus was crazy. He said crazy things like, *"Before Abraham was 'I am'." "Eat my body! Drink my blood!"* If you truly believe, you will never die. You may be put to death, but not a hair of your head will be harmed.

My friends, if you can see it, if you can believe it, Jesus lived in two dimensions. He lived and walked the earth with bones, flesh and blood. He also lived and ruled his life from the kingdom of heaven. He was with us in body, mind and spirit. Being born of God, Jesus could see because he knew first-hand about the kingdom of heaven.

Jesus is a king who is drawing his followers to the place where he lives. His desire is that you abide in him and rule your life with the King of life. Jesus wants you to see with his mind the indescribable beauty of God's kingdom and the heart of the Father. Your Father in heaven is desperate for you.

EIGHT

A TWOSOME

M e and the boys settled in. Jacques began school. Sean and Jaden continued in daycare. Arrangements were being made for Jacques and Jaden to move to Athens. Sean would stay with me. The boys going to Athens did not seem like a big deal. I was there often, and it was easy for them to visit.

Me and Sean became a twosome around Hayesville. It was a pleasure to take him with me around town. We often went to Penland's for the music and dancing. Red and Alvin Ledford were there most of the time. The music was great, and we got in some foot-stomping dancing.

What was God doing in all of this? At the time, I had no idea. I had some prayers out there, and I had asked for the prayers of the Holy Spirit. I had also asked to know Jesus more personally and more intimately. This Spirit was looking at my needs and the desires of my heart which was created in the image of God.

This was not a human heart prayer. Although, I did not understand it, the Spirit of truth would bring me to a place where I could better understand the heart of my Father in heaven. I would be brought to a place of unexplainable, deep, penetrating love. I would see the beauty of God as never before.

God would appoint a small child to teach me. A lot was going to happen in the life of Sean over the next three months. We were just getting settled into a routine when Sean's life was once more disrupted. You will have a hard time understanding what is taking place unless you have been a mother and a father to a child. I was known to the boys as G-dad.

However, I was becoming a mother and a father to Sean. We ate together. We bathed together and we slept together. Sean was on my heels. I did not know at the time, but Sean was a treasure who my Father in heaven had appointed me dominion over. I was everything to Sean. I now wonder if some of his identity is in me. As I was taking care of Sean, I did not understand it, but I was literally giving myself to Sean. In his innocence he was totally wrapped up in me. We were as Forest Gump would say, "two peas in a pod."

Life isn't fair! One day, I went to the daycare to pick up Sean, but Sean was gone. I was devastated. His mother had picked him up. Under normal circumstances this would have been okay; however, I had been speaking with Julia and her partner at the time. I knew that she was being influenced by drugs and the guy that she was with was a complete nut case.

I was mad. I was hurt; I could not imagine Sean being with those two. Please understand my daughter is a beautiful, loving, caring mom. However, Satan had used the allure of drugs to rob her of her true identity. The thief had also stolen the life of the man that she was with now.

What happens in real life when there is a disruption of families is that the child becomes more of a pawn than an innocent human being learning their way in life. As I have tried to see things from Sean's point of view, my heart becomes overwhelmed with the desire for the kingdom of God to come to earth as it is in heaven. For this infant, he is experiencing a normal beginning of life, because it is the beginning of his life. I know this and it breaks my heart when I look back and try to see from the eyes of a thirteen-month-old. I am beginning to understand more clearly what I am praying for when I say, "thy kingdom come on earth as in heaven." What I want is peace, love, comfort and joy for all people including this thirteen-month-old child.

God knew just how to reveal his heart to me. He took the image of his heart and placed it in me, and now he has awakened God's heart that is in me.

One day every knee will bow, and every tongue will confess that Jesus Christ is Lord. That will be the day! As John writes from the island of Patmos; *"The old order of things has passed away"* Rev. 21:4. The old order! There will be no thief. A child can play near the cobra's den and put its hand in the viper's nest. Nothing will harm anyone.

Through my boys and Sean, God has revealed his beautiful heart. With his heart of love, God gave us his Son. This reality has truly been made known to me through the love that God has placed in my heart for an innocent child. One day long ago, I was that innocent child, and the world robbed me of my innocence. Now God has revealed to me, here is a small child in rough waters, tossed to and fro. My eyes were never aware of these things until I was appointed care over this child.

When Sean was not at the daycare, I called the sheriff. I arranged to meet a deputy at the jail. When I got there, there was a representative from social services with the deputy. I had come to get help from someone to go get my boy.

You may think that it is strange or possessive to want to get Sean when he was with his mother. However, I had been on the phone several times with the man with whom she was seeing. The drug induced drama was horrific. At one time he called and said he had no money. He was barefoot, walking on hot pavement in Florida, with nothing on but shorts. Julia had driven off and left him (supposedly).

I called the sheriff. They in turn called social services. Social services sent a representative to check on the environment that Sean was in. In ten minutes, the lady had observed Sean and his environment. Evidently, it met their standards. This made it impossible for me to do anything legally to help Sean.

I knew the situation. I had lived it for a long, long time. Yet, in ten minutes. a stranger to this family, determined that Sean, an infant who was still lacking in his own personal identity, was in an "okay" place. Whatever he saw around him, was Sean's new life and his personal identity was being shaped by dysfunction. For Sean, the life that he was in was his and it was "normal according to government standards".

Sean had a very limited history and very limited experiences for him to use as a basis for what is considered normal. However, the heart of his G-dad was in turmoil. My heart ached for Sean just as I now know that God's heart aches for his humanity.

I believe that Sean's first ten months of life had some good and solid foundational principles. When he was two and a half months old, he was baby Jesus in a Christmas drama at the church, that I pastored. He had heard the songs. He had heard the Word and he had many prayers from the people that he blessed.

His brothers were with him at this little church which was primarily void of children. This seemed to make my boys more special. When I use the term my boys, I do not take away from their parents. It is not my desire to take away from them. Jacques, Jaden and Sean became my boys not out of desire, but out of circumstances. Our lives came together in this vast universe that God created. I did not plan to love them more than others.

What happened was that relationships were developed out of circumstances. Eventually it would be clear to me that I loved Sean more than any other child. This love would not take away from all of my other children and grandchildren. It would be a plus for them as well as every other person I encounter in life.

In scripture there is a verse that says, "*the disciple who Jesus loved*" (Jn. 13:23). This is not to imply that Jesus loved one more than others. To say that would be to say that God has favorites. That would be contrary to the very nature of God. God sent his Son as a gift to the whole world. When

John writes, "*For God so loved the world*," that wording could be changed, and it would not offend John or God. The Bible is not being re-written when I can feel in my heart that God's love for me was (is) so great that he gave me his only Son as a gift to help me overcome the negative forces in my life. God is not a possessive god, (although he is a jealous one. He must be your only God.)

My Father in heaven who gave me his Son is a freeing God. He wants us to be free to receive love as we have never been loved. Love is about acceptance and relationship. Without accepting any person just as they are in life, we cannot have true unadulterated love. Without true acceptance, we cannot have a true loving relationship. Relationships can be negative, or they can be positive. Two countries at war have a negative relationship. A man and a woman who live together and do not accept one another where their journey in life has brought them will have a negative relationship.

Human relationships are giving and receiving. We could say give and take, but that would be counterproductive in building a true, lasting and loving relationship. One cannot take love. First, someone must give it. Then it can be received. True love is the most valuable possession in heaven and earth; however, it cannot be taken by force. It can only be given and received. When it is not received, it is of no value to the one to whom it is given.

Love is that unseen power that does not disappear just because it is not received. When Jesus spoke about sending the Spirit of truth, he said, "*He will glorify me because it is from me that he will receive what he will make known to you*" (Jn. 16:14). What does the Spirit receive from Jesus? Jesus says that this Spirit will reveal all truth. As we look at this verse, we should come to know and understand that the Spirit reveals the ways and words of Jesus, which is the greatest truth known to humanity.

God sent his Son to die because of his love. Jesus proved that this love was truly more powerful than death. What kind of love is this? It is the "fountain of youth" love. It is a love that will never die. It is a love that will never cease to exist. It is a love that cannot be taken away. Not even the death of the physical body can separate a person from this love for even one tenth of a second.

It is a love that you cannot measure. It goes beyond the universe, if there is a beyond. It exceeds the boundaries of time and space. It will carry you into the forever and ever. It will take you to the last day (Rev. 22:5) where there is no time. To experience this love in Spirit and truth is to step into the dimension of God. As Jesus says his words are full of the Spirit and life (Jn. 6:63).

I knew that my daughter Julia loved Sean. However, I was concerned for his well-being. I had no clue at the time, but our relationship was nowhere close to what it would become. Through this child, God was beginning to expand my capacity to love. I had prayed the prayer to be able to know Jesus more personally. I have found that to truly know him is to truly love him.

NINE

TRUE LOVE IS BEAUTIFUL

L ove is used rather loosely in what we call modern life. However, God's love is the most profound love that one can ever encounter. It is more than an "oh baby I love you" because "oh, baby I love you" can be fleeting depending on the circumstances.

Decades ago, I believe that I was fortunate to have begun to fall in love with a fourteen-year-old girl when I was sixteen. We had supervised dates at the gym where we danced. We had picnics. We ran together in groups of other teenagers. We swam at the river and we double dated at drive-in movies. I'll admit that I can't remember one movie. For some reason I remember milk duds! I always had a job and a car, so we got around. It was just a special time for two young people. Our relationship grew. We accepted each other. However, at our ages, it was slowly developing into deep feelings of love. I guess you could call it puppy love, but what is puppy love? I remember riding with two buddies of mine in an old farm truck with a bad passenger door.

We were three young men (boys,) just out for a ride, having a good time talking about girls and really just being alive. It had become quiet. My mind was in a whirl. My heart was pounding. My feelings for this young girl overwhelmed me. Suddenly the door of the truck flew open, and I found myself hanging on. (The window was down, and my arm was resting on the door.) I was hanging on with feet in midair. It really was not a big deal. Tommy slowed the truck, and I swung back in.

Yet, what had happened in my heart and mind was much more significant. As I was thinking about my girl, I felt love at a whole new level. I wasn't thinking about sex. I was not thinking about possessing her. I just felt this beautiful sensation in my heart and mind. There is no doubt that at that moment in time I loved this girl with no strings attached. When I think about our relationship, I remember it as a beautiful experience. It taught me the value of a true relationship versus the emptiness of a shallow relationship.

What is important about a beautiful experience is that you can take that experience and use it as a foundational principle for developing relationships. The spiritual part of relationships is much more lasting than the physical part of a relationship.

God would teach me through Sean what it is like to always be the giver in a relationship. God is a giver. He gives light, life, truth and love without a blemish. He is giving it right now for those who can receive it.

When we receive from God, what we have received is planted in our heart and written on our mind. This is when we have the pure sweet love of God in us to give to others. He has let us know that we have his love within us when we have the ability to love all of God's created children. At this level of love, we become one in Spirit with God.

I believe that God wants you and I to have beautiful relationships in our life. I believe that my youthful encounter with the opposite sex was beautiful, yet it ended during my time in Vietnam. During that time, I had little patience for stateside drama and so my young love affair ended. At the time I had lost all confidence in God and so I was alone in a dark world of death and despair. However, my ability to love and forgive would grow with me, Sean and my boys.

November 11, 2013, I took my sister, Debra, who resides at a care facility, to a Veteran's Day lunch. After lunch was over, I had taken my sister home. I was tired. It was at least forty mountain miles from home. I decided to find a place where I could pull over and take a nap. On finding a quiet place, I pulled off the road, put the seat all the way back, reclined the seat, laid my body back and I was soon asleep.

I think I had a fairly good nap before I was awakened by the sound of my phone. It was Bob Hart, a friend of mine from the Senior Games. Bob is a great, friendly and jovial guy. He is very likeable.

Bob asked me if I would consider going to a ballroom dancing class at the Peacock Playhouse in Hayesville. I told him I had read about it in the Clay County Progress, but I had just never got around to going. Bob said that if he went, he would like to know at least one person who was there, so I agreed to meet him there that evening.

As it turned out Bob was a good ballroom dancer. Me! I was a kick up your heels sort of guy. Just give me a beat that I can match with rhythm, and I am off. Where I am off too, and where I am going, I do not truly know, but I dance. I love it!

I said earlier when I was napping that my phone woke me and that it was Bob. It may have been Bob's voice coming over Bob's tongue and through his lips, however, the call was the beginning of an answer to my prayer. I didn't know it at the time, but Bob was calling to tell me that God himself was setting the stage to introduce me to a person who would be the answer to my prayer for a woman in my life.

When God does things, he does them right. He does them in the best way. He does them for the right purpose. God knew that I did not need just any woman in my life. He knew that I needed the *right* woman in my life. The woman!

One could say that it was just fate or coincidence that I would meet the woman of my life. Faith and coincidence will lead to a woman. However, when God answers a prayer, it will be *the* woman.

I got to the ballroom before Bob that evening. When I went through the door, there was a crowd. Mostly women! There were smiles and giggles. It may have been just my perception, but I believe that I was being examined and sized up like a piece of meat in a grocery store.

Bob arrived. At first, we were just standing around chatting. I do not know how it happened (Bob tells it best), but suddenly we found ourselves talking with two ladies. The conversation was general. Names! Where are you from? How did you find out about the ballroom dancing class? We were still talking when the instructor said to get your partner. Well! The girls were alone! We were alone! So, it was kind of natural that we team up.

When I put all of this in perspective, I see God's hand. While God was using Bob to set the stage, on my end, he was using someone else to set the stage on Maureen's end. Things had fallen into place, and I had met *the right* woman.

I remember seeing something in her eyes that night as we spoke in the dimly lit parking lot. I saw a longing in her eyes. Was it her longing that I saw, or was it a longing that I had for the deep, personal, intimate, passionate and loving relationship for which I was longing, to regain the feeling of myself as that teenage boy who was recklessly in love? I know now that God, my teacher, was bringing me deeper into his life as I received Him more deeply and passionately into my heart.

God's love is like a cool drink of water on a hot day, or a warm blanket and a warm flickering fire on a cold day. God's love is what we need all the time, every day. God would teach me that my deepest longing was to be infused with his kind of love within me.

My Father in heaven knew our hearts when He introduced me to Maureen. He introduced me to the love of my life. Satan would scheme to bring this relationship to an end, but God's angels would run interference as our relationship grew.

---— TEN ——---

THE BATTLE – THE MERRY-GO-ROUND

I t was just a couple of days after I had met Maureen that the phone rang. It was my daughter, Julia. Her mother's instinct had overpowered whatever else was going on in her life. She was concerned for Sean. The man she was with was out of his mind looking for something in the apartment. He was dumping drawers and who knows what else. Julia was worried about Sean. I told her that we had to call the sheriff. My son James, a police officer in Georgia, had warned me not to mess with anyone on drugs. He knew how unpredictable they could be.

Julia put the situation into my hands, so I called the sheriff's office. I can only imagine the scene at the apartment. Having already been involved, they called Family and Children's Services. By the end of the day Sean was back in my hands. I do not recall any real change in Sean. He had only been gone from me for a few weeks.

I do remember having to get a couple approved in September to watch Sean a few days while I went to Raleigh to compete in the Senior Games. I had qualified at the local games for several track events. I guess that my training had been adequate because I managed to take home some medals.

I try to pinpoint times, so that I can paint the best possible picture for you to understand the life of Sean. I had Sean from August 22, 2013, to sometime in October when my daughter picked him up at the daycare.

Now about November 13, 2013, Sean was back with me. It was okay. My next date with Maureen, who I met at the ballroom dance class, was on Friday, and it was in the morning. This was the end of another dance class that Maureen had been in. They were celebrating with a dance class and a light lunch.

Because I had Sean, it seemed that daytime dates were the norm for Maureen and me. We would often go on hikes along the river or mountain trails. Sometimes our hikes involved hiking into waterfalls. There were times that we would take Sean with us to dinner. Then there were times that I arranged for a sitter. Maureen was (is) a real trooper.

We had all come under the watchful eye of Family and Children's Services. Julia had been restricted to supervised visits with me being the supervisor. She could not live in my home with Sean. I am not sure that this did not hinder my daughter's recovery. However, things seemed to be working out. Julia was in Athens, Georgia. I assumed she was working. She had a car. My name was on the financing and the payments were being made.

On one visit Julia spent the night. To me it was no big deal. The next day a representative of Family and Children's Services happened to come by. That was okay with me. I did not object to their visits. However, when Julia came downstairs in her robe, I had no idea of the extent of the drama this would create in the life of Sean. She had not moved in, but they assumed that she had. This assumption quickly led to a round table meeting at the office of Family and Children's Services. During that meeting they informed me that they had taken legal custody of my boy Sean. This was a slap in the face to me. This boy had been under my roof and my protection ninety-nine percent of his life.

When I say, "my boy", I am not short-changing the relationship that Sean has with any other person; however, during all this upheaval, our relationship has been growing. Sean was receiving my heart and my love. In our relationship Sean was returning to me his heart and his love.

Where did Sean get this love so that he would have it to return? In our one-on-one relationship, Sean was receiving from me, and, in turn, he was giving back to me the love he had received. It is like an infant's first breath. Before they can exhale, they must first inhale. Up until birth they receive their oxygen through the mother's blood. Then they are born. At this point they must flood their lungs with oxygen in order for the blood to continue to have life. Blood devoid of oxygen will bring on a quick death.

It is not necessarily how much air you breath in, it is how much your lungs can absorb and infuse into the blood stream that matters.

Like the life-giving blood that is infused with oxygen, our relationship was building. Sean did not have love to give until he was loved. Even then, he could only give what he had received. It reminds me of a Bible verse: *"To those who have more will be given"* (Mat.13:12).

The disciple John writes, *"A person can receive only what is given them from heaven"* (Jn. 3:27).

God has given me an amazing love. It is given from heaven. This love is like being bathed in joy unspeakable. It is love beyond description. God's light from heaven, is the light of love. I know that I have not completely received the depth of this love in my conscious mind, yet I possess it in the spiritual realm.

My love-teacher is still teaching. The student is ready to be taught and the teacher is here. My Father in heaven would use this boy to teach me about his love.

At the round-table meeting, Family and Children's Services informed me that they would physically be taking Sean away from me, another person would be caring for Sean. Sean would not go home with me this evening, and he would be in another daycare. I would not even know where he was.

My fangs began to grow. The hair on my neck stood up. My heart began to beat faster and faster. My temperature rose. Somehow, with God's help, I did not explode.

However, I gathered my senses and I spoke calmly but with authority. I simply said, "This will not stand." They agreed to a visit over the weekend at McDonalds in Murphy. We would have a hearing before the judge in a week, but they agreed to allow me to meet the stranger who would be caring for Sean at Elf daycare that afternoon. The meeting was adjourned. I immediately called my attorney. He suggested that I call an attorney who specializes in this type of case. I called the attorney that he recommended. We were supposed to meet, but it never happened.

I went to the daycare that afternoon to meet the lady who would be watching Sean. She was nice and pleasant enough, but I did not know her. More importantly to me, Sean did not know her. My mind was not clear, but I believe that I had brought Sean the necessities that he would need.

Sean had a wonderful relationship with the people who ran the daycare, but he was glad to see me. We had a routine for meals, bath and reading at bedtime. In between, we always had play time. Sean was always on my heels. Even in the bathroom!

Life dictated that I have more hands on with Sean than any other child that I have helped to raise. I did not know it at the time, but we were like a gift from heaven to each other. God is pretty smart. When you truly want to know him, he will teach you about his heart. Our Father in heaven reaches out with all of his heart to each and every person. Our Father has gone to desperate measures so that we may know him and receive the love of his heart.

The apostle John writes about Jesus: '*In him was life and that life was the light of all mankind* (humans)" (Jn. 1:4). When I went into the daycare and observed Sean, my heart ached. I was deeply troubled in spirit. However, when he saw me, he lit up. The light of God that was passing through me to Sean was coming back to me. It was (is) beautiful.

Knowing the disruption that would take place in Sean's life at this time was more troubling to me than it was to him. I picked Sean up and got his things. He likes neck rides so, I put him on my neck. As we went out into the parking lot, I was feeling the pain of placing Sean into a completely unknown environment.

I can only imagine the heart of God, when humanity, following the human will, abandons the will of God. Now, Sean was not choosing his own will. However, it is humanity choosing their own will that resulted in the circumstances surrounding Sean. Sean was innocent, yet he suffers the sins of humanity.

Here I was going against my natural instinct to protect Sean. By the rule of humankind, I am doing what I did not want to do. Every fiber in me wanted to hold him and never let him go.

Adam and Eve stood at the threshold of human will or God's will. They were created in God's image for a relationship with their Creator. Yet, they used the free will that God has given humanity to separate themselves from God as they abandoned God's will and God's purpose for their lives.

With Sean in my arms, my heart is crying out to God. Your love, your will, your purpose, not mine! I want Sean's life to be right and I am in the place where I know that no life can be truly right apart from God. So, my heart aches. My spirit is troubled.

I put Sean into a stranger's car. I buckled him in. Can you imagine how I felt? Sean had no thought that we would not go home together. There was no resistance by Sean. He trusted me. He could not explain what love is. He could not talk about relationship. However, he loved because he felt love. He was in a relationship with me. He could not explain it, but he knew it and he felt it. How can I explain it?

When you cannot explain something, yet you feel it, what is that all about? I do not completely understand it, but I know, and I feel the love of my Father in my life. How can I explain my relationship with my Father when I, myself struggle to fully understand it?

Jesus says that we must become like a child before we can enter the kingdom of heaven. This means that I must trust God completely when he buckles me in for a journey. Sean trusted me. These days Sean objects when he has to leave me. I ask myself, "Is the world robbing Sean of the ability to trust?"

My heart was aching as I securely fastened Sean into the car seat. On the outside I appeared normal, but on the inside, there was torment, a troubled soul, and a desperate heart. I contained myself as I kissed him, and hugged him, and closed the car door.

Sean's new caregiver gets into the car and closes the door. I stand and watch as she backs the car up to turn around. I just stand there, and I wave as she leaves the parking lot. I do not know where she lives. I do not know what daycare Sean will visit tomorrow. All I really know is that my boy is being taken away.

Can I explain to you how I felt? Try sad! Try hurt! Try confused! Try bewildered! Try upset! Try troubled! Try mad! Must I go on? No one truly knows how I felt. That is because no one can possibly know the depth of love that I had (have) for this child. No one else can know the full extent of our relationship.

What had happened was that a government organization had stepped into our lives and judged this situation based on their knowledge of other situations. Were they right or were they wrong? It is possible that they were right in legal custody? However, they served to only bring further damage to Sean when they took him out of my physical custody. Oh well! It was just a few days until Saturday, and I would see Sean.

Who knows how I felt? Only my Father knows. He knows the pain when Adam and Eve got into the car with the devil as they turn their back on God. Two innocent people were carried away by the promises of Satan (see Gen. 3:4-6). My Father also knows the hurt and the pain of freely giving his one and only Son into the custody of humanity. God's love is what drove Him to desperate measures.

I do not remember the lady's name who kept Sean, but she was somewhat comforting. I got to McDonald's early. I was sitting inside, when the lady drove up with Sean. I met them in the parking lot. We were equally glad to see each other. My heart was warmed just to see him, touch him, and hold him. I can't even remember for sure if there was a representative from Family and Children's Services. I do remember playing with Sean. When Sean was distracted in the environment, I had an opportunity to speak with his new temporary caregiver. She was somewhat comforting.

She told me that Sean was not like some of the other children that were put into her physical custody. She could tell that he had not been traumatized. I can only imagine what some children go through in broken homes where drugs are a part of everyday life. Parents who fight constantly and are substance abusers are often also child abusers. God's heart aches for humanity!

Infants who grow up in a negative environment perceive the life of their parents to be normal. Infants who grow up in a positive environment also perceive that environment to be normal. I am sure that in negative environments there are some positive things. I am also sure that in the best of homes there are also some negative aspects. I believe that it is a parent's unconditional love that can be an over-riding factor in the well-being of a child.

There is a scripture that says children will suffer the sins of the fathers (&mothers). This is not a punishment from God. These are self-inflicted wounds that humanity brings upon itself.

ELEVEN

ALIGNMENT WITH THE SPIRIT

Every movement brings into being another movement. When a sail is pulled into the wind, it creates power and movement. I have done a little windsurfing. When I pull the sail out of the water, it first assumes a neutral position in the wind. This creates a back-and-forth flopping in the wind. At this point I am holding the sail with a rope attached to the mast. To move with wind power, I must pull the sail in, and take hold of the bow which is attached to the mast. Once my hand is on the bow, I have only to pull the sail into a position that catches the wind. As I do this, the board begins to move. First, I bring it into alignment with the wind. As I bring the sail around to catch the wind, the board begins to glide across the water. It is my action that brings into cooperation and alignment the sail and the board. At this point, I begin to surf in the wind. When I bring into alignment the sail and the board, the three of us together produce a movement. Movements of the spirit of a child are produced based upon with whom they are in alignment. For this example, let us use the child, the parents, and the spirit.

In your mind, you can visualize a parent or parents and a child. The outside or the inside force that we all must deal with every day is the spirit. There is a spirit that is in alignment with the well-being of the child and the parents. When Jesus was speaking with Nicodemus in John 3:8, he was speaking about the Holy Spirit, the Spirit of truth that is in perfect alignment with our Father in heaven and with Jesus "The Christ" who God sent to reveal God's truth. This Spirit is active throughout all creation to renew the hearts and minds of all people so that they may be brought back into fold with God.

When this Spirit is at the forefront of the relationship of a mother and father, the Spirit works to help keep them in alignment with each other and with God. When the parents are in alignment with each other and their Father in heaven, the child has a teacher that is the creator of all things.

What a child has when its parents are in alignment with God is the Spirit of truth alive and in their midst. This Spirit produces a love that is impossible apart from God. This Spirit is a spirit of peace and of confidence in the future, regardless of where you are in life. This Spirit produces harmony in the midst of God's creation and in families.

When you are in alignment with God, you can begin to see and experience the eternal dimensions of God. You begin to see beyond your human ability. Jesus spoke very plainly when he told Nicodemus that he could not see the kingdom of heaven unless he was born again (see Jn. 3:3). He told his disciples that salvation is impossible with humans. He goes on to say that with God all things are possible.

Apart from Jesus and the Spirit of truth, it is impossible to come into alignment with God. When you are not in alignment with God, it is impossible for you to guide your child into the way where they can experience the confidence of being God's eternal child.

Prayers for a child to receive God's comfort and peace (the most wonderful gift given to humanity) will be answered when those prayers are in alignment with God's will and purpose.

Although evil things happen to children and followers of Jesus, it is not God's will. However, God has turned humanity loose to do good or to do evil.

While serving in Vietnam, I saw the atrocities of humans against humans. I wondered why God did not stop it, so I turned on God and denied that God existed. I have now come to understand that evil comes from the fallen human race. Real peace and joy, total peace and joy are beyond human ability to achieve.

Jesus said: "Peace *I leave with you; my peace I give you. I do not give to you as the world gives. Do not let your hearts be troubled and do not be afraid*" (Jn 17:27).

When you or I speak of God's peace, we must realize that we are speaking about eternal realities. We are not speaking about a temporary peace and comfort that will fade away. In the dimension of God, we have peace, comfort and joy that the world cannot see or understand. Jesus had eternal peace and comfort as he went to the cross. We must teach truth and eternal realities as we learn to live in alignment with Jesus.

Each day every family must also deal with the spiritual forces of evil. There is a battle even right now in the heavenly realm for the hearts and minds of all people.

When a child lives in a home of disharmony, their hearts and minds are being constantly bombarded by the spiritual forces of evil. This home can take on many faces. Satan is an artist of lies and deceptions that lead to darkness, suffering and death.

Jesus, speaking to the Jews, told them that their father was the devil (see Jn. 8:42-45). These Jews were supposed to be the ones to lead the people into the ways of God; yet, they had fallen into the devil's trap. They were deceived and did not know it. They were blind, but they claimed to have sight.

When a child lives in a home that is not in alignment with the ways of God, Satan will seek an atmosphere in that home that has the appearance of harmony. He will lead you to believe that you can have an abundant life apart from God. He will tell you that you are okay.

What truly makes you okay is for you to come to know the one who created you and of whose image you bear. You have been created in the image of your creator. He is the lover of your soul. He loves you beyond measure even when you are blinded to his truth.

"Jesus wept" (Jn. 11:35)! I am reminded of when Jesus wept. Here we have the Son of God, the creator of all things, the Prince of Peace, the King of Life and yet he was brought to the point of tears.

Why would God weep? Jesus came from God as a gift to humanity. He was (is) a man of many miracles. He demonstrated complete authority over the wind and over gravity. Jesus is God with us. However, Jesus' most used title for himself was the Son of Man. Jesus felt all of the hurt and pain that we feel.

Lazarus, a friend of Jesus had died. He had been in the tomb four days and nights. He was dead. He had two sisters whose names were Mary and Martha.

Jesus risked his life when he went to the aide of Lazarus and his sisters (see Jn. 10:31). When Thomas a disciple realized that Jesus was going to help Lazarus, Thomas said to the rest of the disciples, "*let us also go, that we may die with him*" (Jn. 11:16). So, they went. Upon being greeted by one sister then the other, Jesus asked them, "*Where have you laid him*"? Now, Jesus knew what he was going to do. He knew that this day Lazarus would walk out of his tomb. Jesus, with one command, would undo the decay of death. Jesus had told Martha that anyone who lives by believing in him would never die (Jn.11:26).

Jesus was a close friend of Lazarus and his two sisters. He was a regular visitor to their home. When Jesus saw Mary and the other Jews weeping, it troubled him in spirit. After he asked where Lazarus had been laid, Jesus began to weep (Jn. 11:34).

We could easily say that Jesus weeping was just his human emotions surrounding the death of Lazarus. However, Jesus would soon reverse Lazarus' death.

Scripture tells us that Jesus only does what he sees the Father doing. I believe that Jesus not only saw the Father weeping, but he also felt the heart of God weeping for humanity.

Here were Jesus' close friends. He had come to know them, and they knew Jesus. However, they still did not understand that Jesus was the destroyer of death and the king of eternal life. Jesus had come to model eternal life, and yet they did not understand the abundance of God's gift. The heart of Jesus was breaking. He would give his life just to be understood. Jesus would give us himself completely so we can understand the depth and the power of God's love.

Have you ever been desperate to be understood? Have you ever had a child or known one who is bent on self -destruction? Most of us have seen someone going down a dead-end street. You could talk until you are blue in the face, and it would not help. It literally breaks your heart when someone you love deeply is living a life of self-destruction. You feel powerless, because you are powerless!

God gave Adam and Eve a free will and they used it to say my will, not God's will. So often today humanity says my will over God's will.

JESUS WEEPS – TWO TIMES

As Jesus approached Jerusalem, *"He wept over it"* (Lu. 19:41). Like a child bent on self -destruction, the people of Jerusalem could not see or understand what would bring them joy and peace. God wept. Our Father is reaching out to humanity in love, but He is being rejected. The reason that God is rejected is that people do not know God.

Our Father in heaven is desperate for you. He wants you to truly know him, and he wants to know you. God is seeking a close personal relationship with you. When God sent Jesus, that was a love letter from God to you personally. He will not force a response; however, he will receive you with joy and delight. Jesus is your brother who wants to give you all that he has. The choice is yours.

Back at McDonalds: When the caregiver for Sean told me that he was not like many of the children that she cared for, what she was seeing was that Sean had a peace about him that had not been destroyed. Although Sean had had some negatives, the good had so far outweighed the bad. He was loved by Mom, G-Dad and many others. His recent life was unstable: however, he had experienced over ten months of stability. He had lived in my home. His mother Julia cooked and cleaned for him (baby food). We started Sean on regular food as his system would tolerate. Sean had wonderful people at daycare. What I am saying is that Sean began his life in a way that established trust in his mind and spirit.

The visit was good, but it was too short. When Sean thought that he was going home with me and I had to put him in the stranger's car, he protested as only a small child can. He wasn't defiant. He was many things that he could not understand or explain. He was hurt. He was perplexed. That is, he could not understand how suddenly his life had changed. Sean was put in a foreign land with strangers that he did not know or understand. Everything about his life was different. The conversation, the meals, the bath, the bedtime.

After a bath (shower) Sean liked to be wrapped in a towel and held. Then he was tossed on the bed and bathed in oil or lotion.

G-dad's shower was two feet deep and about four feet square, and I could stop the drain and let the water build up. There were many toys. I could fill some of them and squirt the water. I can see Sean now sitting in the water playing, with his mind traveling to worlds unknown. These were times when he was completely absorbed. For Sean there was no time, just the present! It was always just the present, and he knew what would happen next. He was at peace. However, now as I was putting him in a stranger's car, and he did not know what would happen next. He was being robbed of his peace.

A HURTING SEAN

I can see his face now and the tears of a little boy who was hurting. He was a little frightened. Why is G-dad putting me in this stranger's car? Why is he doing this to me? You see, Sean had questions in his heart that he did not know how to explain. When he couldn't talk, how could he say, I don't want to go? How can he say, "I don't like this?" Can he say, "Explain to me what is happening?"

I felt his hurt. I felt his pain. And, like Sean I was doing something that I did not want to do. I was buckling a bewildered, teary-eyed little child into the car seat of a stranger. I would have to close the door as little arms reached out to me. I would have to let him go. My heart was breaking. I could only imagine the bewilderment and hurt in the heart of this ten-month old.

I backed away from the car as I looked at a sad little boy with tears running down his cheeks. I cannot explain my feelings at that moment. Love for a child. Hate for this situation. Anger! Resentment! I cannot tell you the tears that I have cried and the pain and hurt that I have felt or the prayers that I have prayed. There were two little boys in that parking lot that day. They were both hurting. Great love brings great pain. That is the price of loving and caring. The student is ready to learn, and the teacher has appeared. My heart was breaking just as God's heart breaks for all of his created children!

I had asked God to know Him more personally, more lovingly and more passionately with total freedom to fully experience the love of God.

As the car drove off with the apple of my eye, the one God gave to my love and care; I hurt in an unexplainable way. Sean was alive. He was safe. I would see him again (Lord willing).

At this moment I was the other little boy. I could not understand or accept this. Yet, I had to. My God, my God, why is this happening?

Humanity has chosen their own will and purpose. Long ago we abandoned the ways of God to seek our own will and purpose.

When God sent Jesus, he gave us a way to right the wrong. He gave us a way to come home to our Father. He gave us a way to have the peace, comfort and joy that overcomes pain, sickness, suffering and dying.

How can I know this way? I must first know God before I can see the way. God knew my heart that day as the car carrying Sean, one of my treasures, pulled out of the parking lot. The teacher was there.

To know God is not to know about God. To truly know God is to move into his heart. To know God is to be born of God. Just as I was in pain because of love, I know now that my God suffered and died to rescue humanity. I was desperate for peace and comfort for my boy Sean. God is desperate for all humanity. He loves so much that he gave us his heart. That heart was (is) revealed in a man called Jesus.

I could have cursed the world because of what was happening. However, I had prayed to know my God and my Lord Jesus Christ more intimately and more personally. It was (and is) a prayer of my heart. Jesus promises us that if we pray in his name, it will be done.

It is important that we know that when we pray in the name of Jesus we are to pray for God's will and God's purpose. Then we must trust and obey. There is no other way to be happy in Jesus.

Jesus promised the Spirit of truth would come to teach those who are prepared to receive God's truth. The truth of our Father in heaven is grounded in the foundation of love.

Standing there in that parking lot, I felt the anguish, sorrow and the pain that Christ endured because he loved without condition. He asked for forgiveness for his tormentors. Nothing inflicted upon him overcame the heart of God's love that was in him. It was in my broken heart that he revealed this love to me. I began to feel the unconditional love of God flow through me like a river. It is unexplainable and I know that you cannot experience it unless your heart has moved into the heart of God.

THE BATTLE

I had called an attorney who had been recommended by an attorney friend to represent Sean in the upcoming court hearing. With time being short, we never managed to get together.

The morning of the hearing, I began to prepare for battle. I got in a quick workout just to get the blood flowing. I showered. I ate a light breakfast with coffee. It was a cold morning.

I put on tights and a body shirt for warmth and comfort. I put on a crisp white shirt and black slacks. My shoes were black and buffed. I wore a knee length wool jacket, and I adorned my neck with a camel hair scarf. As I went out the door, I put on my black leather gloves. At that time, I had a Marine Corps haircut. I dressed for intimidation and battle. As a Marine, I knew how to dress with the appearance of authority. I wanted my boy Sean's representative to be sharp and intimidating.

I got to the courthouse early. I removed my pistol and other items that I could not take past the screening from my attaché. I entered the courtroom looking like a New York lawyer.

In the courtroom were the representatives of Family and Children's Services along with a person who was to be Sean's voice. It is important to note that I am not against these people; however, we have conflicting views about how Sean's life was to be lived during this time of turmoil.

I went up and greeted the representatives of Family and Children's Services. I knew the person who was to be Sean's voice. However, there was yet another unseen person who would be Sean's voice. I had prayed that the Spirit of truth would prevail and speak through me. Upon the greeting, it became apparent that my dress and my persona had its desired effect. I was not just some other person – I was Sean's G-dad who prayed to the God of life.

It is quite amazing when the Holy Spirit is at work. As I looked around the courthouse, I saw the attorney with whom I had conversed over the phone.

Where was Sean while all of this was taking place? What was he thinking? By this time Sean was in his new daycare. It makes me think about the night that I met my wife, Maureen. The stage was being set on my end. I remember the conversation with Bob and what led up to me arriving at the Peacock Playhouse for a ballroom dancing class. What was happening on Maureen's side of the stage?

What was happening was that the Holy Spirit was setting the stage to answer my prayer. It would turn out better than my prayer. Instead of just a woman in my life, I would meet the woman for my life. If you remember after my prayer for companionship, I suddenly found myself with a stranger (the stranger was the homeless man who I took in), my daughter and her two boys in my home. I did not know at the time; however, another stage was being set for me to have a deeper relationship with my Lord, my Christ.

Sean may have been in the daycare, but the Holy Spirit was at work on his behalf. I went up to the attorney and I asked if I could speak with him. We went out of the courtroom and found a place for a little privacy.

We briefly discussed the situation with Sean. I inquired about the cost of handling this case. I do not remember the exact figure; however, I believe that it was about a $2,000 deposit to start. With time being short, I asked him if he would sit in with my pre-court hearing. We agreed on a nominal fee. He would sit with me while I stated my case for my boy Sean.

The stage was set. The Holy Spirit had assembled the players. Sean had no idea about the battle taking place on his behalf. I knew that the battle was God's. There was no personal vendetta.

There was just a desire to bring Sean home to familiar faces and surroundings. How many of us have a longing to go back to a place and time when things seemed so right? Pictures of people and places flash before my eyes. They appear as perfect settings. My mind tells me that I was at peace.

I see a family gathering on Sunday afternoon. The sun was warm, the grass was green, and grandparents were sitting on chairs on the lawn. People milled around and we (the children) just ran and played. There was no tomorrow. Just the present!

I see another day. I can see a beautiful young girl with a broad smile and a gleam in her eyes. She appears to me full of life with beautiful expectations. My mom had fixed a great meal. We were a family and this beautiful young girl seemed to fit right in. She brought brightness to the gathering. At least in my mind! She was my girl. We had dreams of a life together, but the world would steal that dream and it would vanish as a vapor. However, on that day life seemed just right and it was for a moment in time.

I could go on, but the day that seemed so right was Sean's day. What will he remember sixty-seven years from now?

Life is just a flash. It is just a breeze that will soon disappear. So why do I have this longing in my heart? I can remember Sean coming down the stairs dragging his blanket. My wife Maureen and I are sitting on the couch. I look up and Sean just gives me that look.

It is not a look of disrespect or disobedience. You see Sean had been put to bed, but now he was up, and he was headed down the stairs. I knew his look. I felt his look. It said, "I want to be close to you. That is where my heart is." He was not speaking words through his mouth. He was speaking through his heart and his soul. Sean has a natural hunger for the closeness that he has experienced. His home is not in a place. It was at this time in my heart. It was in the closeness and the relationship that we have with each other.

Jesus says that before you can enter the kingdom of heaven, you must become as a little child. He also says that the kingdom of God is within you. The kingdom of God was coming down the steps that night. The heart of a little child was coming down the steps that night. His life was not complete apart from the one who loved him. How could he know that it was God's love pouring through the heart of his G-dad that he was drawn to?

Are my longings like the longings of a little child? I believe they are. There is something deep within my heart and soul that thirsts for a time of peace, harmony and love that exists without reason. Am I longing for the day where peace, love, and complete confidence in life eternal will manifest itself when I am at home with God? I believe it is our Father in heaven who can and will satisfy our longing to go back to a place where we are at peace with God.

BACK IN THE COURT ROOM

In the courtroom the role had been called. Then Sean's case was called. We would adjourn to the back room for mediation. Sean knew nothing about what was taking place in this drama of life. He was totally unaware that God was coming to his rescue. Can we possibly know how many times

God has rescued us when we had no idea that his hand was upon our life in a mighty way?

There are so many times that I have been rescued that it would take a book to fully explain. It mattered little to me whose prayers were being answered on that fateful day when God's angel pulled me from the river in Vietnam. What matters to me as I look back is that God had his hand of protection on me. I believe now that he had a purpose for me. The longer I live the more my confidence in God, my savior, grows. I believe that God was answering a prayer that day in the courtroom.

As we went into the back room, my Father gave me an air of confidence and peace. My battle was not for self - it was for Sean. My battle was not to lighten my burden. It was to increase my burden and lighten my heart. I would ask to be the caregiver for a thirteen-month- old boy. For a period of time, I had been his mom and his dad. Before you can possibly fully understand our relationship, you must first experience it. It is not that Sean is any more special or any more precious than any other child or grandchild. It is that we have formed a one-of-a kind relationship. There had been times that it was just me and Sean.

Sean had gone to the square in Hayesville with me. I had danced with him on my neck. I had tossed him up. I would swing him around. He had ridden in the grocery buggy. He went with me on some dates with Maureen. Our relationship was like a grain of corn planted in the spring. It had sprouted and began to grow and grow.

If you can visualize our relationship, maybe you can understand your relationship with God. Through Sean, I could see how desperate God is for a personal relationship with me. When Julia was at the house, Sean was more at a distance. It is not that I did not interact with him and his brothers. It is not that I did not love him and his brothers. However, there was an unexplainable difference in a typical role where you know your grandchildren versus a close personal one-on-one relationship in which you are the sole caregiver.

As human beings, we have very few close and personal relationships. This relationship with Sean is like no other. It is not something that you can decide. You cannot create that which you do not know. My Father was using this relationship to introduce me to the kind of relationship that He wants with me.

Like Sean, I had no idea what God was doing. I did not plan it, nor could I! However, I had asked to know Jesus more personally. God was answering the prayer as Sean began to play on the strings of my heart like one plays an instrument to produce beautiful music.

God is so amazing. Through an innocent, helpless child, God was revealing his heart that He had given to me. I am learning that God's love produces pain. It produces a longing for life to be right and beautiful. I could have turned my back on Sean, but I would not. I could not. I began to see more acutely the love of God for humanity. This lesson from God was a lesson about love.

There was a time when I had turned my back on God. More than that, I had denied that he even existed. I was a young man serving in Vietnam. The world was dumping on me. Death was creating a darkness I did not understand. Today, I wondered what Sean was thinking when he seemed to be abandoned. He wasn't abandoned, but he did not know or understand that the world was dumping on him

Sean did not know that I would die for him. Neither did that young man in Vietnam know that his God would die for him. I had abandoned God, but God did not abandon me. I had no real idea that God would die for me.

Just as God could never abandon me, I could not abandon Sean. Sean had my heart. Little did I know that my Father in heaven had my heart. You could say that I had not given him my heart when I was in Vietnam. That is true just as it is true that Sean did not know that he had my heart.

You might say that Sean was (is) the apple of my eye. Well, you and I are the apple of our Father's eye. He is our creator and our ultimate destiny. One day we will go back to God as we move forward in life. Why not go back to God today and be his blessed child?

In the inner chamber of the court there was a large table and chairs. There was the DFCS attorney and three representatives of the Department of Family and Children Services. There was a guardian-ad-litem, me and the attorney with whom I had spoken earlier.

I did not know if my presence along with an attorney who was known for his expertise in family matters was intimidating to the DFCS attorney or not. However, the DFCS representatives seemed to be emboldened by the presence of their attorney.

They stated their case for removing Sean from my home which was also the only home that Sean had known. It was truly his home. It had not only provided shelter and warmth; it was the base for his life.

From the time he was two days old, my home was Sean's home. It was a place of peace and comfort. His mother, Julia, attended to his needs. From food to clean clothes and diapers, his mother attended to his needs and that included middle of the night needs.

With three young boys it seemed that she was awakened about every night. I would hear the cry of a child and then a mom consoling and taking care of the need of the moment. She often did breathing treatments for Jacques who had a touch of asthma. Julia met Sean's demands for food even in the middle of the night.

As soon as Sean could crawl, he wanted to get in the large shower. We would stop up the drain. With numerous bath toys, bath time was play time. Except for washing the hair, it was a very pleasant experience for a child. This was Sean's one and only home, and I knew it. It mattered to me that Sean's life, through no fault of his own, was disrupted. My feelings were that DFCS added to this disruption.

How was God teaching me through all of this? When I looked back and saw the many times that my life was totally disrupted by the people and circumstances around my life, I knew that anything contrary to good for me was not of God.

The life of Jesus was full of disruption because of the evil that had come into the world. It came and still exists because humanity seeks its will over God's will. Like Jesus, our Christ, it is still the innocent who pay the price for the fall of humanity. Through Christ, our Father in heaven has righted the wrong.

In that hearing I was the caretaker, I was the father and mother of Sean. I was there to right the wrong. I wanted to stop the thief who was intent on robbing my boy Sean of his peace and his home from birth. That day God revealed his heart that was in me to me.

I was not there for myself. I was there for Sean. God did not send his one and only Son to earth for himself (see Jn. 3:16). The Father sent the Son and gave his Son to me, Sean and all humanity who would receive him, believe in his name and use the power of one born of God to be molded into the image that all humanity is created to be.

As I would go into battle for Sean, my Father had waged war and was waging war with the spiritual forces of evil as he taught me about himself and his true nature. I loved Sean as much as I know love which now enables me to receive and understand that God's love is beyond all human knowledge and ability.

I had not thought about it nor planned what to say, but I had spent time in prayer about it. When I opened my mouth, the heart of God in me began to speak. That heart cried out for the wrong to be made right. It was the love of a father and mother who was taught of God.

When God is asked to rule in a situation, his words come out in love, in passion and they are beautiful. God is powerful, beautiful and loving and I was privileged to have his beauty, his passion and his love cross my lips as I waged war against the spiritual forces of evil.

When I finished speaking, DFCS asked for more time to settle Sean's case. With a competent attorney by my side, my Father emboldened me. The Spirit of truth had beautifully set the stage for Sean. I looked at the

DFCS attorney as I spoke for Sean. I simply said that Sean needs to come back to his home. The attorney addressed those present as he said, 'If this goes before the judge, the judge will want this boy back home *yesterday*.'

Home! Home! Regardless of your experience of home, God's home is full of love and beauty. God wants all of his children to come home to him *yesterday*.

The decision was made. Sean would be back home with me today. I do not believe that anyone in that room had any thought that they were not looking out for Sean's best interest. However, in times of family problems, what is right for a child can be distorted. Decisions are often made without true understanding of the effect on the heart of a little child who is at the mercy of those over him. *Today* God righted the wrong.

TWELVE

MOVE INTO LOVE

God gave us his one and only child, He also placed his love in that child. This love relationship would prove to have more power than death. Jesus would prove that life exists apart from the body. His words paraphrased were, I will lay my body down and I will take my body up again. Jesus existed before he became a dot of life in the womb of Mary.

Jesus had said; *"The flesh counts for nothing. The Spirit is life"* (Jn. 6:63). When Jesus spoke about eating his body and drinking his blood to have life, he was speaking about the greater life and the Eternal life which is his Spirit. This is the Spirit of the Eternal God that is in him. When a person receives this Spirit, you are receiving God's evergreen Spirit into a temporary body of flesh. This is no longer a mystery for those who live in Christ.

To live in Christ is to receive his Spirit in you. Then he takes you into himself. In Christ, we find that we are truly at home. It is his Spirit that brings peace, comfort, joy and confidence in the outcome of this life.

For Sean, it was my home, the place of his beginning, which brought him peace, comfort, joy and the confidence that life was going to be okay.

Just as I wanted to bring Sean back home to reassure him that he was not abandoned, and that he was deeply loved, I know now that my Father in heaven wants me in the place where I am loved with a love that this life can never take from me.

That evening I met Sean's temporary caregiver to pick up Sean and bring him home. I can still recall his face as I began to unbuckle his car seat. He was happy to see me and I him.

Had he been robbed? I do not know what the past few days had done to his confidence. He was innocent and helpless to make his own determination as to where he would go or where he would stay. For now, I just wanted to take Sean home to a familiar environment and to love him just because Sean is my boy.

Father, you are a wonderful teacher! I now know that you love me because I am your child! Just as I give myself to the well-being of Sean, God gives himself to my well-being, just because he loves me.

I now know that my Father in heaven loves me with all of his heart, with all of his spirit and with his soul and mind, which is in Christ.

God has brought to me an innocent, helpless child. The love of God is a reflection of the image in which you are created. This love of and from God has created a bond of love between me and Sean. Although Sean could not explain this, he knows within his heart that we are connected because of our relationship that is rooted in the unconditional love of God. This love is so broad, so deep and so high that it is a mystery to the human mind.

Without knowing how, Sean and I are joined by a spirit connection that can be felt, but not explained by a child. Yet this bond that is more powerful than death exists equally between a little boy and a sixty-seven-year-old man. It is equal because it is created by the Spirit of truth that bears witness to our relationship.

My Father in heaven is teaching me that I am his boy. He is teaching me that he desperately wants me to know that I am loved by him. When our Father gave us Jesus for humanity to do with as we pleased, he gave us all of his love that we are willing to receive. It is his natural love for humanity, but from the human perspective it is extreme supernatural love. For me, this love is no longer supernatural. It is the power of God-infused love that flows through me. It is the natural power of God to love in the face of all offenses. God's love is natural and powerful.

It is not supernatural for God. His natural love is holy, meek, nurturing and protective. It is male and female rolled up in one. When you encounter him, your heart is touched in such a way that it melts like a block of ice pouring out of you and you are able to pour into an innocent child who receives it with a smile, a hug or a kiss. You can know without words, that the child receives you. As my love pours into Sean, it is pouring back into God. My Father is teaching me how desperate he is for his love to pour into all of his creation. He has given me a taste of a love of which the world is in desperate need. Now I know, through a little child, how my Father wants me to love all humanity.

If love is to be a burden, let me embrace that burden completely the way my Christ has embraced it. Jesus loved his enemies with all of his heart, with all of his mind, with all of his spirit, and with all of his strength. He loved in the power of God's love. It is my prayer that his love will flow through me like an unstoppable river to all of God's created people. If the love demonstrated by Jesus "The Christ" was in every human being, we would see the face of God throughout the world, and the world would be at peace with God and one another.

As I write these words, my heart is so full of longing. I can see the image of Sean. I see the fleeting moments of time as he moves through the house. A lot of times he has a blanket in tow. I see him coming down the stairs dragging a blanket. He is so quiet. I am not sure if I sense his presence before I hear him or see him out of the corner of my eye. There are so many ways that the world begins to rob the innocent of peace and of love.

When Adam and Eve were deceived into choosing their will over God's will, I can see the earth. I can see the animals. It is as if suddenly a lion eating grass lifts up its head and suddenly has a desire to kill, and the lamb is bombarded by fear. The entire earth begins to groan in the pain of death. The whole earth has been robbed of Paradise.

I pray that my boys, all my children as well as all humanity, will come to realize that the thief is among us robbing us of the abundant life God intended. I pray that all eyes will see that Jesus has come to lead us back to God's paradise, the garden of pleasure and delight.

I am sitting in my living room. It is the close of a day. I am sitting with the gift. That is, I am sitting with the woman that God sent me. I am in the mood for private time. There is a flickering fire in the wood stove with a glass front. It's cozy, warm, and I really like this woman. This is our quiet time. I have no idea what we were talking about when suddenly I knew that we had company. I looked up and there was Sean.

Was Sean an interruption? Yes! However, there are so many times that I have looked up and here came Sean easing down the stairs. At the time I had no idea how rich those moments were.

Me and Sean settled back into a regular routine. He remained in daycare at Elf. This gave me freedom to function in God's ministry and handle some real estate. I became a licensed broker in 1971, and my investment eggs were all in real estate. A lousy real estate market from 2007 up until recently kept me juggling things to keep the taxes paid and stay afloat.

I was dating while I had Sean back in my home. I had met Maureen at the ballroom dance class at the Peacock in Hayesville. It was Bob Hart with the senior games that encouraged me to come to that first class.

Maureen is a massage therapist and at the time, worked for several spas. She was constantly checking her phone. Most of her work was Friday and Saturday which made it fairly easy for daytime dating. Our first date was at the end of a line dance class which she was taking.

Our second date was a six-mile mountain hike to the summit of Siler Bald. She is a trooper and seems to love hiking. We had numerous adventures along rivers, and up and down mountain trails. We have hiked to numerous waterfalls.

There were times that we had to cut a date short so that I could get to the daycare on time. It was a beautiful time. I had met the woman who my Father had sent me. I was loving her more and more each day.

I believe that all true love comes from God. I was getting a double portion of my Father's love. I was delighted in this woman and Sean had become the apple of my eye. He not only followed me around, but he also began to mimic the things that I did.

I have learned that if I am to truly follow Jesus, I must begin to mimic his life. To do this I must begin to love beyond human ability.

Human ability to love is based upon the love that you have received from others. The baby is born. It must breathe in before it can exhale. This can be proven by science. Before the baby is born, its life is dependent upon the oxygen in the blood of the mother. It is alive within the womb receiving life from the mother.

Upon exiting the womb, the baby is still connected by the umbilical cord. This cord which is a conduit for oxygenated blood will no longer supply the oxygen rich blood that sustains the baby's life. It begins to receive its oxygen by breathing it in by itself, a natural process!

It has been said that love makes the world go around and it implies that love is essential to life. The apostle John writes that because of God's love he gave us the life of his one and only Son. He further states that in him is life. For the apostle John, God's love is essential to the kind of life our Father in heaven wants for all of his children.

Our Father knows that the human definition of love is incomplete and lacking in purity. Our Father knows that each person's definition of love is based upon the kind of love that they have received.

As humans, we give love or anything else out of our storehouse of what we have received. My wife Maureen often tells me; "I cannot give what I have not received".

Most of us have read about the disciple whom Jesus loved. The apostle John uses the term love several times more than all the other gospel writers.

There is no doubt that I had (have) a greater bond of love with Sean than any of my other children or grandchildren. This does not mean that I love the other children less. What it does mean is that there has been a closer, personal and a more intimate relationship. Circumstances had a lot to do with this. However, the most important thing was that Sean was receiving and I was giving, and Sean was giving back from the storehouse of what he had received.

My friends, when the King of love and the King of life begins to teach you about love, you begin to melt inside. Something beautiful begins to take place as God pours his love into you. Being born again is the beginning. The breath of eternal life comes into you the moment that you are willing and ready to receive it. With this breath comes God's love.

The love of God is pure and untainted. My Father in heaven had instilled his love into me because my heart was ready to experience the beauty of God's love. The bond between Sean and me came at a time in my life when I was having a beautiful love affair with my Abba (Daddy).

When Julia and the boys came to live with me, I really did not know how deeply God was working in my heart, mind and soul. Being born again is never a done deal. It is the beginning of a transformation, my friends.

When a seed is planted in the ground, it is just a seed. Day and night, it is in the ground. Then it begins to sprout and grow toward the light of day. Who can truly explain it? Through no effort of its own, the seed sprouts and begins to grow.

When you are born from above, the seed of all the attributes of God comes alive within you. You are given the power and the right to become God's child. This transformation begins to take place as you begin to nourish this seed of God in you. The more you nourish it, the more it grows.

However, for you to nourish that seed of God, you must receive nourishment for that seed from God. Unless the nourishment comes from God, that seed cannot, and it will not grow.

When we think about this, it is contrary to human thinking. How can one nourish this plant that came from the seed of God? You do not, of yourself, have God food. This seed is not God. It is a seed that comes from God, and it is his gift to you that can empower you to be recreated in the image that you are created to be.

To those who have will more be given and to those who have not, what they have will be taken from them. In the parable of the talents, it was the man who produced nothing, who had the one talent given to him taken away. These words from Jesus should not be a mystery for those who are born of God.

For the seed of God planted in your heart to grow in the ways of God, it must be the purity of God. God gives you the seed and then he gives you food for the seed. The more you receive, the more He gives you. For God's work to be accomplished through you, it must be accomplished by his Spirit working in and through you.

LAUGHTER

As I begin to notice how Sean would try to mimic me, I begin to realize that Jesus was teaching me about true discipleship. To be a true disciple I must learn to function and live in the image of Jesus. This means that I must begin to reveal the true nature of God.

Is laughter a true nature of God? When God told Abraham that he would have a child at one hundred years old, Abraham laughed (Gen 17:17). When Sarah heard from one of the visitors that she would have a child at ninety years old, she laughed to herself (Gen. 18:12).

Sarah denied laughing, but the angel said, "*Yes, you did laugh*" (Gen. 18:15).

When a son was born to Abraham and Sarah, they named him Isaac. Isaac is a noun which means he laughs. True laughter is real joy. For me it is representative of true joy. I often find myself in joyous, bold laughter in my private times with God as well as in corporate times. Laughing out of the joy of life is a gift from God. In laughter the Father sees in us the joy of life, and I believe that God laughs with us.

One evening Bob Hart and I had a double date at my home with the ladies we met at the dancing class. One of those ladies, Maureen, is now my wife. It was a covered dish affair. The meal was good and pleasant. I believe that Bob may have brought an apple desert. At this moment I cannot be sure about anything we ate. However, the food of fellowship was beautiful and delightful.

The meal was about over, and the conversation involved sharing stories about life. Bob was in the middle of a story. He was having a good time telling it. It must have had some humor because around the table we were all laughing joyously. As Sean joined in, we began to witness his exuberance for laughter. His expression of laughter brought on more laughter. It became intense laughter. All inhibitions around that table were dissolved. Uncontrollable laughter controlled the atmosphere around that table. Sean became the star of laughter. I have a smile on my face this second from just thinking about it. It is unbelievably freeing. For a moment, I am back in the midst of joy and laughter. That night, Sean, was the cheerleader for laughter. Matthew writes in 21:16, "*From the lips of children and infants you, Lord, have called forth your praise*".

I am not saying that we were in a religious worship service. What I am saying is that as a born-again child of God, I believe we were in the midst of bringing joy and delight to our Father in heaven. Just as I delight in the joy of an infant or a child, my Father delights in my joy.

To relegate God to religious dogma is allowing Satan to rob us of joyous and intimate times with God. His children are one hundred percent his one hundred percent of the time. God is life, love, joy, laughter, and he is delightful.

Around that table was delight. I was delighted in the joy and laughter that was dramatically enhanced by a small child. As I delight in Sean, I know that my Father delights in me.

The exuberant laughter around that table wasn't over. It extended to what I call painful, doubling over, belly laughter. We laughed until we hurt. I suddenly reared back in my chair brought my right arm up and without thought (brothers and sisters, I was in the midst of spiritual joy) I brought that hand back down on the table with a bang.

We were already beside ourselves when Sean seeing my joy and my exuberance without warning came around with his right hand and banged the table. He was thirteen months old. I didn't think that we could laugh any louder or harder, but we did. It was Sean's laughter that kept us going. He caught on quickly. When he realized it was his actions carrying the night, he lit up. I have never in my life seen a child light up like Sean. He would laugh, look around the table at the laughter and he would laugh all the harder. In my life this may have been a marathon of laughter.

The laughter slowed, but it had not stopped when Bob said he would like to finish his story. We all had a story, but the real story that night was about the gift of laughter. God said that through Abraham's son Isaac (he laughs) that he would have descendants more numerous than the stars. "He laughs" (Isaac) was born to Abraham when he was a hundred years old. Your Father in heaven helps you through pain and sorrow. He also delights in your joy and laughter.

Religious people often delegate to God a portion of their life. A follower of Jesus, a true disciple, invites God to be a central part of all his life. The God I know is full of life, joy and laughter. He wants to bring us back from what we have allowed Satan to steal from us through deception and lies to a place of joy, dancing and laughter.

Eve did not have to reach out and take the forbidden fruit. Adam was right there. He could have stopped her. However, they were tempted into seeking their own will, and their own purpose apart from God. We see this in life when a child is disobedient to his parents.

In the garden, Satan began his conversation with cunning and with lies. Deceit and lies are a death warrant in a relationship. Our Father in heaven has sent us truth, light, life and laughter. Jesus has promised those who receive him, believe in his name and follow him that they will one day be with him in Paradise.

Isaiah writes, *"The wolf will live with the lamb, the leopard will lie down with the goat, the calf and the lion and the yearling together; and a little child will lead them. The cow will feed with the bear, their young will lie down together, and the lion will eat straw like the ox. The infant will play near the cobra's den, and a young child will put its hand into the viper's nest"* (Is. 11:6:8).

My boy Jacques believed (believes) this. He has even asked me about other animals. Humanly speaking, this sounds like a fairy tale when, in reality, this is describing the Paradise of God when the world and all its creatures and all its people will live forever in alignment with God.

Our Father in heaven, through Jesus "the Christ," has made a way for us to return home with all of our rights as an eternal child of God. Our Father God has undone the wrong and He is wooing you to come back into his arms. He has a robe of righteousness, and He wants to put the ring of his eternal love on your finger. Live the joy of being God's child, and let laughter rule your days.

CAN YOU DO WHAT I CAN?

Try as I might, I cannot fully wrap my head around Sean. What seemed to please Sean most was to mimic me in the things that I do. He was content in being with me.

He was with me shopping and on some of my dates with Maureen. All of the boys loved Maureen from the beginning and Sean was no exception.

One day I was preparing to put a new liner in the trash can. I had a particular way of opening the bag. One day as I unrolled and unfolded a new liner, Sean was there. He wanted the liner. I relented and gave it to him even though I wanted to get this chore completed. He took hold of the bag. Then he began to shake it up and down wildly. I thought to myself. What is he doing? Then it dawned on me. He was doing what I always did. Even Jesus said that he does what he sees the Father doing. I was the only father this little boy knew. I was the example for him. Little boys cannot properly grow into young men without a male role model.

Sean shook that trash bag with abandon. That is what I did after I got it unfolded. When I shook it, I was pulling it through the air. As the air went in, it would open the liner. This sometimes took a few good shakes. When I realized what Sean was doing, it delighted me. He wanted to do what I did. It did not really matter what it was that I did. What mattered was that Sean a very small child wanting to be like me and do what I did. This is the very reason I want my boys to get their eyes on Jesus. He is the lover of their soul and a perfect role model.

Followers of Jesus should have a true desire to do things the way Jesus does them. We should learn to love and forgive the way Jesus does.

CHRISTMAS

By Christmas that year (2013) Sean was fourteen-and-one-half months old. The week before Christmas me, my brothers and sisters participated in a family ritual of getting together for one big family gathering. There are eight of us. When counting the children and grandchildren plus a few friends, we have a large gathering.

For the first gathering, everyone was at Moms. My ninety-year-old grandmother was there. So, were the great, great, great grandchildren. This gathering is now over thirty years old.

I brought Sean and Maureen to Christmas 2013 at my brother Dale's house and Reico, the boy's dad, brought Jacques and Jaden. It was a huge gathering. Reico tried to keep the boys off me, but they wanted to be swung around in circles and ride on my neck. Jacques was all smiles and Jaden had that shy smile. He wanted you to see him, but he doesn't want me to know how much he wants my attention. He can melt my heart.

It was a memorable night. My brother Dale was out back on the lawn with lots of guys and kids all over the place. There was a little beer drinking, a lot of laughter, and sharing of life stories. Dale was doing his tradition, grilling marinated venison tenderloin wrapped in bacon. It is the crowd favorite among a hundred other dishes. I can see the faces and the smiles and the children with an anticipation that lights up their faces. It is that special time of the year.

We are celebrating life whether we know it or not. This is a celebration of a birth. Do we really know what this birth is all about? This birth is God's gift to humanity to bring us back into alignment with God. For those who can see it, we are celebrating the eternal life of Christ which our Father in heaven wants to bestow on all of his children.

Christ is life eternal, and he will transport us even this day into an eternal celebration with our Father in heaven. Our family gatherings are beautiful and memorable, but they are passing away. I yearn to live in that feeling of joy and unity when a family gathers to celebrate life in the place that Jesus promised he is making for us.

Jesus is a life that is not passing away. It is his desire to lead you into the eternal realm of God, where there is joy, dancing, laughter and complete security.

There is a story in the bible about a son who left his father and wasted all the wealth that the father had given him. When he returned to the father, the father did not lecture him but received him with joy. He immediately prepared a celebration with food and laughter and music.

When we come home to our Father, there will be a celebration. There will be laughter, joy, music and dancing.

THIRTEEN

INTO HIDDEN TREASURES

eing involved with the woman with whom God had put me, I was very busy from Christmas until spring. Although Sean often accompanied us on dates, here I was at sixty-seven years old and in need of a babysitter at times.

With a flexible schedule, Maureen and I often had day dates. We walked mountain trails to high peaks. She would go with me into hidden waterfalls that over ninety-eight percent of the population in Clay County has never seen. I remember bending a small tree over a creek so that she could walk across to stay dry while I bent another tree over for her to hold on to.

On that day, we had gone into an area that did not have a trail. Where the trail ended, we worked our way through thick laurels to a beautiful waterfall that I had often come to as a boy. Hot House Creek flows across a mountain of underlying rock on its way to Shooting Creek and Lake Chatuge. The water went from steep cascades to vertical descent.

The water seemed to welcome the fall. It tumbled and splashed against the rocks, full of joy as it enthusiastically tumbled into a pool at the base of the rock wall.

When we got in close to the base of the waterfall, there was a ledge where the water hit several feet above the base. Over the centuries, the water has carved out a pool in the rock. From that pool the water pours over the ledge where there is a larger pool of water.

We found a place to sit on moss covered rock. This was in the early stage of our dating. The conversation was pretty generic, but the atmosphere was exhilarating. It was cold, but we were dressed for cold, we were warm. There seemed to be no urgency to leave this spot. It was enchanting. It was story book.

We could see the water rushing over the cliff. It was falling rapidly, and at the same time it created a symphony of music. There was the sound of the rushing water through the air, of the water landing in the pool. It rushed over the second ledge into a larger pool. Then, the sound of the creek coming to the first ledge, and of the rushing water continuing down the mountain. We were listening as we were breathing in an atmosphere that would never be duplicated again. The waters were in harmony along with the surroundings in tune with the water. There was mountain laurel in such abundance that we had to bend and sometimes crawl to get into this isolated waterfall.

Now I get it. My Father had brought this woman to me and somehow, some way, the Spirit had led me to invite this woman to walk with me to mountain crest as well as into the heart of the mountain. We had also walked along river trails. Sometimes on a drive we would just stop along a creek or river just to see, hear and feel the beauty and power of God's creation.

As we ventured into places of beauty and unity which our Father had created, I began to see more and more of the loveliness and poise in the woman that God had brought to me. She is humble with a quiet boldness. She is delicate yet daring. She ventured with me even when we had to make the trail. It would not be long before I would ask her about a permanent relationship but for now, our relationship filled a void in a man's life. There is something beautiful and new taking place in the life of a sixty-seven-year-old man.

This man was falling in love with a grandchild to whom he was a mother and a father and was falling in love with a woman like never before. What was happening? What was God doing? God was teaching me about his love and how He would provide for me all things, if I would allow him.

God was answering prayer in more ways than one. I had asked to know Jesus more personally. I had asked God for companionship. With his lessons, I was becoming part of Jesus more intimately and more personally.

My Father went deeper into my heart and inner longings to answer my prayer for companionship. My logical mind was seeking companionship based on my experiences in life. However, my experiences were limited. My heart truly wanted the companionship of a woman with whom I could be in unity and alignment. My Father knew what I needed. Had I not asked the Spirit of truth to intercede in prayer for me? I had. In so doing, I was asking for my Father to intercede. I am promised by Jesus that if I truly pray for God's will and purpose, my prayers will be answered.

As I have come to know Jesus intimately and more personally, he has given me a larger and deeper capacity to love. Some would say that it is supernatural love. For me, that is an attempt to put God on the human level. When something takes place that is beyond human ability and capacity to understand, we are tempted by Satan to call it supernatural power of God. In so doing, we miss the fact and the reality that in Jesus "the Christ" we see the natural power and love of God. We see the hidden treasures within us.

God does not suddenly do something that is beyond his natural ability. The teachers of the laws of God and the Pharisees asked for signs from Jesus to demonstrate that he had what could be called supernatural powers. Living in deceit, they could see Jesus and the miracles of God, but they were so deceived that they were too blind to see.

What began to take place in my life is nothing short of a miracle. It is not supernatural for God to answer prayers. God looked into my heart. He knew that I did not have the experience there or the capability to pray for fulfillment of the longings deep within my soul. When I became free enough to pray for God's will and purpose to be accomplished in my life, it was as if the Spirit nudged me and said let me pray for you.

My friends, it was not as if the Spirit nudged me, the Spirit *did* nudge me. I am still learning to be aware of the presence of God at all times in my life. I have to admit that this makes me a little uncomfortable. How about when you go to the bathroom, or get into bed with your wife with things of the flesh on your mind? I like to think that there are times that God pulls down the shade.

You see, I have come to realize that I need God all of the time. If someone had a hidden camera, I am sure that when I am by myself you would catch me saying excuse me, pardon me, and forgive me. I am not nuts, but I truly believe that God is always present in my life.

I know God will be there to take my hand when the cold darkness of death approaches to lead me into the eternal light of his love. I died with Jesus long ago and I have risen with him to live forever as a brother of the eternal King of life.

God Himself has written his laws on my mind and he has put them in my heart. When his law of love is in your heart and written on your mind this is when you begin to truly walk with Jesus. You mourn with him, and you begin to love as he does.

You come to know that to walk with Jesus, is to live as one who overcomes the world. When you live the forgiveness of Christ, you embrace the hidden treasures within you. For a follower of Jesus, forgiveness is not an option.

FREE TO LOVE – FREE TO HATE

Since God does not require you to do anything but demands to have all of you, you are free to choose. He loves you too much to control you. He wants to have a close intimate relationship with you too much to put controls and limitations on that relationship. Through Christ Jesus you are set free. Free to love! Free to hate! Free not to forgive, or free to forgive.

Our Father in heaven has given each of us his heart to do with as we please. When he sent us his one and only Son, he gave us Jesus completely. Jesus, the servant King gave all that he had. In so doing, those with eyes to see, can see that God loves you with all of his heart, all of his mind, all of his soul and all of his strength. All our Father asks of you is to freely love him back. From there begins the fulfillment of all of God's laws. When you truly love God, you will learn to forgive as God has forgiven you.

My Father set the stage when he placed Sean in my care and introduced me to Maureen. I would experience the innocent love of a child, and the heart of a woman who was being molded into the image of God. Through the unconditional love flowing through the hearts of these two people, my capacity to receive and give love would grow. I began to see through the loving eyes of Christ. It is phenomenal when love touches you with greater depth than you have ever experienced. There is just something about the electrifying love of God. As it comes into your body, your mind and your spirit, your life is lit up. It is like a charge going off within the depth of your soul. This charge travels through your entire body, your mind and into your spirit which is full of a life that will never end.

That is, the essence of God's love has come into your entire being. You are completely restored. You are being molded into the image of God. You are becoming the image of God that you are created to be. You are more than a mortal being when you have received Jesus "The Christ" into your life. Who you have living in you is the eternal Spirit of truth and life.

Jesus says that to have life, you must eat his body and drink his blood. To fully understand these words of Jesus, you must be born of God. When you are born from above, you are born out of love. God made this birth possible through his love revealed in his one and only Son. Our Father in heaven loved us so much that he gave us himself. The eternal life of Christ. Jesus is your invitation to a deeper love.

God's love is like rain coming down from heaven on a dry and thirsty soil. It is the essence of God flowing into the heart and mind of all who will receive it. It is beautiful. It is passion. Let it flow into your heart. Let it fill you to overflowing so that you may experience the depth of love as never before.

FOURTEEN

THE BOYS LEARN TO SKI

Spring was coming. Jacques and Jaden were coming to visit me and Sean. There had been enough cold weather for Beach Mountain, N.C. to have their slopes open for spring skiing.

It was March 2014 and my Father had given this sixty-eight-year-old man the fortitude to plan a ski trip with a seventeen-month-old in diapers, a three-year-old soon to be four, and a five-year-old who would be six in May.

Many a time, the boys would be boys. All three were in car seats, all buckled up in the back seat. I often had to adjust my mirror to look in on the disagreements and fussing in the back seat.

We had played games of counting cows and horses. This did not go very well since their counting ability was limited. Sometimes, we would see who could first spot an American flag. Occasionally, I would find some music to their liking and they would do a jig in their car seats.

There was a little bouncing with extreme arm and shoulder movement. This was okay for a while. Then their arms tended to get into each other's face. Of course, Sean was low man on the totem pole. That is, he received more than he could dish out.

It is interesting that this brotherly fussing goes all the way back to Cain and Abel. It got so out of hand that Cain killed Abel. No wonder jealousy is such a powerful tool of evil. It drove Cain to kill Abel. My boys love each other but they could become jealous at the least thing. I mention these things because I believe that it is extremely important to recognize evil in its infant stage. Jealousy is evil.

Jealousy may have been the reason that Adam and Eve disobeyed God. The serpent promised them that they would become like God. They were created in God's image. However, when they choose to follow Satan to elevate their will over God's will, they led the human race into the darkness of death.

Our Father is even now a loving parent who gives us a free will. We can choose life, or we can choose death. You may be thinking that we are all going to die. That is true only from the human perspective. From the spiritual reality, when you make a place in your life for the Father and Son to live, you become the temple dwelling place of God. In God there is no death. You could say that even Jesus died. That is only true from the human perspective. The Spirit and life of Jesus laid his body down. That same Spirit and life took his body up again. As humans, we have a very narrow and limited vision. Through the eternal spirit we have an ever- increasing vision of life as we begin to see through the eyes of Jesus. When his Spirit lives in you, you possess the Spirit of the eternal man, and that Spirit will never leave you.

I knew that it was from jealousy and boredom that the boys were fussing. They were jealous over the bag of craisins, and they were bored. My nerves are usually pretty good when it comes to children. However, being confined in a car seat with no way to burn the stress energy (fight or flight energy), I was getting a little uptight. The boys were expelling some energy with teasing and fighting and crying. I began to think; man, you are crazy! You are out here alone with three small boys. You are no spring chicken and you have still got an hour and a half to ride. Are you crazy or what? When you begin to talk to yourself without opening your mouth, you are getting into trouble. Since you can't hear what you are saying, you can't be sure of the tone. I decided that I would verbalize my thought to the boys. If they heard a new and different tone from me, they might listen.

Knowing that they may have been subjected to loud arguments, I decided that I would speak in a humble but direct tone. I first had to get their attention.

Boys: Listen to me! Listen to me! Settle down and listen to me. You are going to get into trouble. Okay? Do you see those trees that we are passing by? Do you see those limbs on those trees? If you do not listen to me, I am going to stop and get me a switch. You know what that means?

When I began to slow the car, as if to stop, it suddenly became quiet. Then I said look at me in the mirror. When I had their attention, I said to them; boys you know that you are with a crazy man. There is not another man in the world my age who would load three small boys in a car to go skiing. Not one of you can ski. Am I not crazy?

The older boys seemed to sense something. They settled down for a little while. That was all it took. Being still for a little while was all it took for them to fall asleep. They became angels in my eyes as they slept.

I'll never forget how my Father blessed me with my boys. I adjusted my mirror so that I could feast on the sight of them. They were beautiful. They were innocent. For this period of time, they were my Father's gift to me, and I was my Father's gift to them. In our relationship we were blessing God. And I am the apple of my Father's eye. It is such a privilege to be guided by my Father's love.

When the angels of God rescued me from death several times, God knew that one day he would give me innocent children to teach me about himself and his great love.

Loaded with rifle, backpack, grenades and gear, I was sinking for the last time in a Vietnam river and God rescued this non-believer. Malaria took away forty percent of my weight in a few weeks. I left my body, but God saw fit for me to take it up again. The landmine tore me from heel to throat, but God brought me through it all. I have faced death up close and personal, but my God has revealed to me my never- ending life.

As I look at the boys, my heart melts for them. Now I know that the heart of my Father in heaven melts for me. He sees me in my innocence. He loves me completely. The Spirit of truth is an awesome teacher for those who become aware of the unseen presence of Christ in your life. Look at the Boys! They are beautiful! They are asleep! There is this unimaginable power filling me. It is the power of God's love. I know that I am receiving love, and I know that love is being received. **That is the electrifying connection of love.**

When you plug in a lamp, you plug it into power. The power is there all the time. However, until the lamp is plugged in, it cannot receive the power. I am so glad to be plugged into God!

As I look at the boys, my love covers them. I no longer see the envy and jealousy. I no longer see the fussing. I see beauty and I see love. My Abba is love and the Spirit is the conduit that connects us. The connection begins with Abba and the Spirit is the wind that transports the love of God directly from the heart of God. His love is conveyed through me to my boys.

We arrived and finally made it to our room. It was one large room and a bath. We would eat, bathe and sleep. I had brought lots of healthy snacks of nuts, seeds and dried fruit. I brought a five-pound bag of craisins which the boys were especially fond of. There was always a debate about who held the bag. After things settled down, Sean had worked in his turn to hold the bag. I can see him right now in his diaper walking around the room munching on a bag of craisins.

I felt like the boys needed a real meal. To my displeasure what they were determined to have was pizza. I relented. After all, this trip was more about them than me. I decided then that on this trip I would be with them as much as is reasonable. What that means is that I would allow them to choose as much as possible as long as it was reasonably healthy choices.

Jacques was determined to have the pizza his way. I decided to let him have half of the pizza his way. I believe that Jacques wanted a cheese pizza. I decided that we would go to a place less than a mile away and eat at the restaurant. Sitting around a wood picnic type table, we ordered our half breed pizza. When the pizza came, I expected Jacques to dig in to it. What actually happened is that he didn't eat one piece. Jaden and Sean ate a little and I had a couple of slices with a beer.

One could say that the pizza was a waste. That is how I felt at the time. However, as I reflect back, it was the event of getting pizza. It was the event of allowing Jacques to have some say in his life. I realize now that the real food was in the time God gave me with my boys.

When Jesus fed the five thousand men plus women and children, it was not about the food. Yes, they all ate their fill. However, the food would vanish into history, but the abundance of God's love and his generosity is a table that God has prepared for those who love him. Pull up a chair and feast on God's banquet.

As I sit here, write and remember, I see love. I see generosity. I see an abundance of love being poured out on three small boys. I now know in my heart that it would be impossible for me to give as freely unless my Abba (Father) teaches me to give. It is God in me that loves through me as I become a gift to God simply by allowing his great love to pour through me. It is a washing of love. It is a cleansing of love. It is being immersed in the unexplainable love of God. It is so beautiful. It is so indescribable that it cannot be explained. To understand it and live in it, you must experience a love sent from heaven. When you receive this love, and believe in this love, you are born a new person who is being filled with this beautiful, unconditional love that is raining down from heaven.

My friends, it was not just pizza, three boys and G-dad. It was Jesus, pizza, three boys and G-dad. No one can set the table like the Spirit of God's love. Pull your chair up to the table and eat. Just as when Jesus said, *"This is my body given for you"*. He is saying to me, he wants me to have the keys to the kingdom of heaven and access to all that he has. I stand amazed at what God has done. Jesus truly is a light to see into the abundant life. Sharing life and the taste of fellowship with my Father is beautiful.

Back in the room it is a little chaotic. I decide on sleeping arrangements. There is one bed. Jacques will sleep on the couch. Me and the other two boys in the bed. During the night, Jacques, who has a touch of asthma, began wheezing. I grew up asthmatic and know how it feels. It was a tough night for me and Jacques. I do not carry any medicine except maybe aspirin since my heart surgery. We struggled through most of the night, but eventually his breathing calmed down.

I believe that knowing what it felt like to struggle for breath may have made it a little harder on me than on Jacques. When his breathing settled, he still had some wheezing. He would be sleeping while I was fretting. We got through the night with reasonable rest.

I had already decided that we would choose all day skiing. By doing complete days, we would have the option to ski on our schedule. To be in a rush with three small boys could become stressful.

On rising, I changed Sean's diaper and made coffee. We ate cereal, dried fruit and nuts. Sean was hanging on to the craisins. We were fortunate that the weather was mild and sunny. The packed snow was groomed, and the slopes had few people.

I got the boys dressed for skiing and Sean packed for daycare. When we arrived at the Beech Mountain parking lot, I would check Sean in at the daycare center and change into my ski boots. I carried the backpack with snacks and extra clothing in case we had the need to dress up or down. Sean was accustomed to daycare and the young lady was very friendly. She quickly got Sean's attention focused on the toys, games and other children.

In addition to the backpack, I also had to carry my own skis and I was continually giving the boys neck rides. I knew that I would not need an additional workout at the end of the day.

We went to ski and boot rental for the boys. The boys were bright eyed and great. They had seen people skiing. I imagine they thought that they would just get on these skis and ride. They were very adept with wheels and skateboards. The boys were soon fitted and ready to go.

Afterward, we went to get our lift tickets. Jaden was free. Jacques was half price. The next day I learned that seniors were half price. For two days I got half price entrance.

The first thing that I did was take the boys to the top of what I call the bunny slope. I got the boys locked into their skis. I first had them move their skis from side to side. I had them make a vee wedge in the front. This is sometimes called the snowplow position. In this position you create a backing action when you tilt the skis in. This can give beginners control of their speed on the downhill slopes. My objective for the boys was to teach them how to control the skis. We went through a series of letting the skis begin to slowly move down the slope. At first when they got a little speed, they would just sit down. Eventually, they learned the snowplow which would stop them rather quickly on the bunny slope.

The bunny slope was fairly short. At one side of the slope was a cable with bars that had a hand grip at the base. The next challenge was to grab the bar and point the skis uphill. Done correctly it was an easy, quick pull back to the top of the slope. It took several trips for the boys to master the proper technique.

My next objective for the boys was to learn to turn and stop without snowplowing. This was somewhat challenging. In skiing when you shift your weight to the right ski, crouch a little and lean left while making the left ski light (meaning little pressure on that left ski), you will begin a left turn. When you become parallel across the slope (meaning you are not facing down slope, you are facing across the slope), you can apply more pressure on the right ski and come to a complete stop.

The objective to control your downhill speed is to continually shift your weight, as if doing an easy up and down motion, as you shift your weight. To stop, you simply carry the twist to a hard right or left or you can choose to ski at an angle down and across the slope.

The first day we stayed on the bunny slope. The boys progressed quickly. Jacques began to try to go in and out of the cones positioned on the slope for the purpose of learning to turn. They both mastered the bunny slope the first day. However, Jacques was adapting to the turns more quickly than Jaden.

At the end of the day, we went to pick up Sean. When I went in to get Sean, the daycare lady brought me some of his clothes in a bag. She said, "You may want to throw these away." It turns out that Sean had a major clean out, a blow out, complements of an overload of craisins combined with one of his favorite foods which I had brought, sweet potatoes! He had probably also had some of my flax seed mixture that I always have for breakfast. Anyway! The lady said that it was a major clean up. That fiber stuff really works.

As I was headed back to the car with the boys, we saw a lady in a wheelchair. We had seen her earlier that day and she was fascinated with the boys, especially Sean! Just seeing the smiles and the energy from these boys was like a banquet for the spirit of this woman. They put a broad smile on her face and her eyes were lit up. She was aglow in her fascination for the life and beauty that she saw in these boys.

I knew that we were connected in spirit. So, I asked if my boy Sean could give her a kiss. 'He sure can' she said. Laying my skis down, I took Sean off my neck. I asked him if he would give this woman a kiss. Then I leaned over with Sean in her direction. Sean seemed to love the attention from the lady. They connected. There was no coaxing. When I got him close enough, he leaned toward her and kissed her right on the cheek.

A precious moment in time. Six people. The woman, her assistant, three boys and G-dad. Who set the stage for this beautiful encounter? My friends, when prayers to know God more personally are being answered, it is not an accident. That moment is etched in my mind. For a moment in time, six people were in alignment with God, fulfilling the purpose of God to love one another. Be on guard, my friends. God is looking, watching, not to judge or condemn, but to celebrate this love with you and those you meet along the way.

The next morning, we got to the slopes late. We were up and down the bunny slope. Jacques was working the cones. Jaden was doing well, but he liked being close to me. When we took a snack break and came back out, the lift was not running. No one was around. I looked at the lift for the beginner slope. It was much steeper than the bunny slope. However, if you skied across the slope, it was fairly easy. I had two boys who had about six hours on the bunny slope. Here goes!

"Boys do you see that lift? We are going to ski to the lift. This being your first ride, I will ask the attendant to stop it for us to get seated." We skied to the lift and got in a short line. When it came our turn, the operator stopped the lift. We boarded. At the top. I signaled to the operator to slow the lift. I told Jacques to ski one way and I would assist Jaden in the other direction. Jacques made it fine, and I guided Jaden. We got away from the lift. I told Jacques that he could ski across, but he had to wait for me and Jaden.

Jacques made his first stop, and I came along with Jaden between my legs. Jaden was better than he realized; however, he chose to stay close to me. After the second stop, I told Jacques to go for it. He was mastering this slope. Jaden stayed with me. Jacques lapped us many times that afternoon and the next day.

The boys thought that I have skies that will ski uphill. They did not realize that I was just enhancing my work out by pushing uphill to get back to them at times. I think that I will let them figure out the uphill skiing on their own!

Although I wore a hat, we all got a little sunburn from the reflection of the sun on the snow.

BEAUTIFUL CARGO

At the end of the last day, I loaded my skis and boots along with the boys into the car. It would be a quiet ride home. We stopped for some food, then returned to the car. The boys did not last long. They were tired after three days on the slopes and Sean seemed to be tired from playing. He was used to it being just the two of us most of the time.

The boys quickly fell asleep as I began the four-hour drive home. I was tired but pleased about the trip. It was challenging, but two boys now had the gift of skiing.

For the moment the boys were at peace. Who can know what they were thinking as they dozed off? Looking in the mirror I could see three beautiful children asleep in a car seat. Their trust in me to get them home safely was apparent. Their trust in me alerted my senses. I drove tired but ever mindful of the precious cargo.

There were moments when there was no past, no future, just the present. If I had to describe the atmosphere in that car, I would say that the car was full of love. I did not have to reason or think about it. I just loved these boys. During these quiet times, I could see their beauty and their innocence. True love is completely out of control. It comes easily, it can't be forced. You connect with it. Love just reveals itself on its own and becomes a driving force within you that must be released.

From where does love come? Where does it go? I am in this car. I am the one awake and the overwhelming power of love engulfs me. What can I do with it? I can do nothing with it. Love flows on its own power.

In describing the Spirit to Nicodemus, Jesus uses the wind metaphor. He says, (regardless of human interference,) the wind blows wherever it pleases. Jesus says that the Spirit is like the wind flowing freely. Love must be in the wind of the Spirit.

Love that I feel flows around me and through me into the atmosphere. We are taught in scripture that the word of God never returns void. There is no other power that reveals God's word and God's truth that is greater than God's love. Love never returns void when it is freely given.

It was in the power of love that our Father in heaven sent Jesus. Love came down in the flesh. The apostle John says that the Word became flesh. He further states that God so loved the world that he sent love (Jesus) through the Spirit of life as a gift to all humanity.

I am driving down the road. I am headed home and my heart aches with the pain of love. I see my treasures in the back seat of my car and I know that I love them with all of my heart. Whatever they do! Whichever direction in life that they take. I will love them. I have them but for a moment in time. My love wants to cover and protect them.

My prayer is that one day they will know this God of love who will always love them. Regardless!

For tonight, I am privileged to carry a precious and beautiful cargo. I am also aware that I have company. The Spirit of truth is riding with me. It is the presence of the living God who has come to be my teacher. I now know that just as I adore and love these boys, my Father in heaven loves me and he adores me. What is more, I trust him to never, never part from me.

I am so glad that I have allowed the God of life who adores me to make his home with me and in me. I am the eternal child of God, and I want my boys to come to know the wonder of this King of life. I want them to be his blessed children. I look back at three beautiful, slumbering creations of God and my heart overflows with the adoration and love that my Father gives to me.

My wife, Maureen, often says that she cannot give what she does not have or what she has not received. Before a newborn baby can exhale, it must first inhale. Our ability to love is based upon the application of the love which we have received. That is why it is so important to love those with sincerity who seem to be unlovable. My son, James, a policeman, is often asked why he treats those that he has arrested with such kindness. He says that his words may be the only kind words that they have heard in a while.

FIFTEEN

MY BOYS – A FIRE, CREEK & MARSHMALLOWS

Back at my place we rested, but not for long. Within a day, I had invited Maureen over. Our dating had begun over four months ago. She had become a very important part of my life.

I built a fire out by the creek. The boys like to get sticks out of the fire and make disappearing shapes in the dark. It was like drawing on a chalkboard with an eraser close behind the chalk. The faster they moved the stick in the darkness, the more lines they could see before they vanished.

Marshmallows were the focus. Eating them was a small part of the roasting. I would cut some green roasting sticks, and the boys would roast a few and burn a few. I would never allow the roasting to begin before we had a good bed of coals. A lot of times we would combine marshmallows with graham crackers and chocolate to make s'mores.

There was just something special about hearing the constant flow of the water, a warm fire and having a boy hanging on your knee. We were not thinking of the past or the future. We were all wrapped up in the present.

The boys would always get around to popping mountain firecrackers. Green leaves from the mountain laurel would create numerous popping sounds when thrown into the fire. The fire, the creek and the boys were a combination that blessed my soul.

Back in the house, I had a fire going in our wood heater with glass doors. I had pulled out a workout mat to cushion the floor. It spread out to about four by eight size. Me, the boys and Maureen laid down in front of the heater. The five of us were lying close together. I am not sure when it happened; however, there was a bonding with Maureen and the boys.

That night on the mat I could not touch Maureen. When I did, Jacques would move my hand. At the time he was five years old, and he had staked his claim on my girlfriend. In a very short period of time, the boys became very close to Maureen. I believe that it had to do with the unconditional love in her heart. I also believe that it was and is the connection with the Spirit of truth.

God's love was in the atmosphere that night. The student was ready, and the teacher appeared. I believe that God brought five lives together that night, with no thought about it nor human effort, a bond was created. Our Father knew each heart and he was writing the law of love on those hearts.

God's greatest purpose for any human being is to be able to receive and give love. As my heart becomes more into alignment with God, I can with trust and confidence pray; 'Father Thy will be done in my life and in the lives of those I love.' The greatest attribute of God is love. And, He wants every person to know and believe they are truly loved with a love that not even the death of the body can take from you. We are more than flesh and blood.

ADVENTURE – DAILY GRIND

The next adventure for me and the boys with Maureen would be St. Patrick's Day at the Daily Grind in Murphy, NC. To me the Daily Grind is like a family pub. They serve sandwiches with accompaniments along with beer, wine or most any other beverage. On Wednesdays, Fridays and Special days they have music.

It was St. Patrick's Day, and the Daily Grind was all decked out. When we arrived, it was apparent that we had come into a party. There were green hats, green pearls, green balloons and almost any other kind of green you can imagine. The music was lively and other children were present. We danced and cut up with the boys. We ordered drinks and sandwiches and got a good table (that is we were in front of the band).

It was a beautiful free atmosphere in the Daily Grind. Kids were running around, dancing and having a good time. They were quickly adorned with St. Patrick handouts. I lost my phone with the pictures of Jacques and a little blond girl under our table. Sean was right in the middle of them.

My teacher was still teaching. There have been times in my life when I would have never thought about God on an outing to a pub with drinking and dancing and just celebrating life. Why would you put God out of the picture when you are celebrating life? We were enjoying pure wholesome fun and sometimes acting like children. The boys were having a good time and so was I. We danced our own dance to the rhythm of the music, and we let life unfold.

When God has become a central part of your life, He goes where you go. God's dwelling place is in the heart of those who receive him into their lives' and who truly believe. It is from receiving and believing that faith is developed. It is through receiving God into your life that you become a child born of God.

When I look back and see the faces of these boys and Maureen, I see a beautiful, joyous occasion. I also see two people (me & Maureen) bonding in truth.

Maureen can see the life in the boys and the life in which they bring into relationships. I can see her acceptance of the boys as she gets a better picture of who I am. Her delight in the boys gives me a better picture of this woman who God has brought into my life. I now see that out of what seems to be a chaotic and challenging situation, God was creating beautiful relationships. We received the positive atmosphere at the Daily Grind. In return, we added a positive contribution to the atmosphere. The newborn must inhale before it can exhale. As we breathe in the positive atmosphere of the celebration, we begin to exhale into the atmosphere the positive vibes that we received. We all danced the dance of life, and my God is life.

THE PROPOSAL

Another fine evening, Maureen and I returned to the Daily Grind, I believe that Sean was with us. Jacques and Jaden had gone back to their dad's.

In the past I had asked her to marry me. Marriage to Maureen was a real big thing. I know that it should be a real big thing to anyone. However, it was a bigger thing to Maureen. She was fifty-seven years old, and she had never been married. She was waiting to make sure that it was the right thing to do. Maureen was not comfortable talking about marriage. We had met about four and a half months earlier. Again, we were sitting in the front of the pub by the windows.

There was a flaming heater near where we sat in a living room like atmosphere. Music was playing. Sean had become a hit in the pub. He is a naturally outgoing child. For a time, we were regulars at the Daily Grind. We were sipping on a drink. The atmosphere was warm and cozy. Even though it was cold outside. We were sitting by a fire in a cozy setting and the warmth had come right into our hearts. The Spirit of love was truly present. The wind of the Spirit was truly moving. Who can know where it comes from or where it goes?

When God is the conductor of an important event, where he is answering prayers, you best believe that he is present. He has written the script that is in alignment with him and two hearts. He is not forcing the issue. He is helping to implement the prayers of the Holy Spirit that is the heart's desire of one's soul. I have asked the Spirit to pray for me in ways that are far beyond my personal experiences in life or my understanding.

In order to know love in a greater depth, you must be taught about love beyond your current understanding of love. I stand in awe of God's love and yet I have not truly reached completely the depth of God's love.

It was an awkward moment. I can see us now. I see the gleam in the eyes of Maureen. I see a longing that I cannot grasp or understand. If I wait until I understand the longing, I know it will be replaced with a deeper longing that reaches into the depths of one's heart and cries out for the eternal peace of God for all people.

I was thinking about marriage to Maureen. I was thinking about asking her again. I do not know exactly how it happened. I was prepared to debate the issue. However, I am not sure that I was completely prepared to receive a positive answer.

As I have been searching to more fully understand marriage, it has dawned on me or been revealed to me just how sacred the bond of marriage should truly be. First, God has proposed to be a husband to his people, which are those who accept him and believe in his name. Without a complete and true unity of the Spirit there is not a true marriage. Our Father in heaven, proposed to you a one-sided marriage of which he will always be faithful regardless of what you do.

When you stray from God, he is always quick to forgive you and receive you back. It is like the amazing story of what we call the prodigal son. When the son was returning in disgrace and unworthiness, the father saw him in a distance. He did not stand around and watch him come begging. The Father did not walk, He ran to embrace him and reinstate him.

Your God does not wait to condemn you. He does not wait to judge you. He is waiting for you to see that life is better with your Father than without Him. He is waiting for you to come to a place in your life where you can receive his forgiveness. The father of the prodigal son was living with the inner pain of a son who rejected him. He had allowed him to leave and take with him the assets that he had accumulated with his father. He had squandered those assets.

Now he was returning. The world had whipped him and robbed him. He no longer felt worthy to be called a son. He was like a dog with its tail between its legs whimpering and hesitantly returning hoping to be able to live again as a servant because he felt unworthy to be called a son.

The heart of the Father, on the other hand, is forgiveness. Forgiveness is central to the nature of God. The Father forgives freely. However, it can only be received by a repentant heart. God does not keep you from cleaning up your life. He is standing by ready to help you. My friends, you are forgiven. Can you accept this forgiveness from God so that you can forgive yourself and allow God to become your partner for life?

God has made a proposal to you through Jesus "the Christ". Jesus has paid the price and he is asking you to receive his life. On bending knees, Jesus bowed down before humanity when He washed the disciple's feet.

When his prayer to the Father while hanging on the cross was received by the Father, it was a done deal. Jesus said, "...*It is finished.*" (Jn. 19:30). It is complete. It is a done deal. When he asked the Father to forgive you, forgiveness was complete. This is the one-sided marriage of God. He loves you regardless. He forgives you completely. However, until you have accepted this forgiveness and change, the weight of sin will rob you of your life. The infant must receive air to live. Forgiveness is a done deal. However, until you receive it, it is of no value to you.

The father in the parable of the prodigal son did not stop loving his son. He always had his heart and mind open to receive his son back into his home. When the son was in the distance, the father recognized his gait. The father knew that he was returning to him, and he ran as his heart melted within himself. He ran to receive him. Before the son could speak the words of remorse, the father embraced him. He loved him. Regardless!

In the Daily Grind, Maureen and I sat looking at one another. I was a bit nervous. I was also prepared to debate Maureen's objections. I do not remember the exact words, but the Spirit must have nudged me at the right time. I asked Maureen to be my bride. It startled me when without hesitation she said "Yes; I will be your bride." At the time I had no idea what this truly meant. Of course, I knew about marriage, but I did not know about a marriage that God was putting together.

What I am saying is that my Father was answering my prayer to know Jesus more intimately and more personally. As a marriage comes into alignment and into unity with love and respect from each person who accepts the other persons journey in life, we begin to exhibit God's love in us by the way that we love and respect each other.

When God becomes the center in a marriage that center keeps bringing us back into unity when the evil spirits continually try to divide us. It is in a loving marriage that we learn to recognize when the atmosphere begins to become negative between couples.

In a marriage, the human mind and body, become cold as the atmosphere becomes negative because of a disagreement or misunderstanding. Believe me, the devil can convince you that you are right, and your partner is wrong. They do not understand you. They don't seem to care. Have you ever had these kinds of thoughts? Believe me, evil is speaking division and distraction to your mind.

Jesus said that instead of peace, he was bringing division. At first this seems contrary to the objectives of unity with each other and God. However, look closely at his words. Jesus brought division between the ways of God and the ways of the devil.

That negative atmosphere that comes into relationships is from the devil. He uses his knowledge of what will light a fuse or conduit to blow up and detonate a relationship. On the other hand, the Spirit of love and truth brings a positive atmosphere of seeking to understand your spouse or friend. Your Father in heaven is asking you to seek to understand his ways and the ways of your friend before you try to have your ways understood.

When two people enter into a growing relationship with each trying to understand the other, there is a lot of positive energy that produces a deeper bond and a deeper love. Your Father in heaven wants his children to have the best possible relationships. The devil is set on destroying relationships. There you have the division which Jesus, "My Christ" speaks about.

Jesus brought division all right. His ways were so different than the fallen human nature and the ways of Satan that he was often said to be crazy, or demon possessed. Jesus' life reflects the ways of God. He demonstrated the love of God. The apostle John writes that God did not send his Son into the world to condemn the world, but to save the world.

The father of the prodigal son did not condemn his son. His son suffered self- condemnation because of his choice to live apart from his father. The division that Jesus brought is the division that is the difference between the ways of God, and a fallen people living in separation from the Father.

Children of God come to know and recognize the spirits. They know the Spirit of truth and love. They also recognize the spirit of evil and discord. We all must decide which spirit we will allow to guide our lives.

At the time when Maureen said yes, I had no idea of what God was truly doing. He had seen the need of these two hearts and put them together. He would teach them to grow in love and understanding. Only God knew what we truly needed. He knew that we needed someone with whom we could be united as we together seek the will and purpose of God.

As human beings we get caught up in this thing called control. We do not even like having to use self-control to control our speed when driving on our roads and highways. We primarily give into this control to avoid tickets, fines and high insurance. Forget about safety. We are more concerned about controlling the cost of fines and high insurance cost. We know that highway safety is enhanced because the roads are patrolled, so we yield to self-control of our driving habits.

With God there is no control. He did not control Adam and Eve in the garden, and he is not seeking to control you. Jesus said that he came to free the prisoners. Jesus did not open the door of human prisons. He did not enter into battle with Rome. He did not endorse a human kingship like David's. He was not a military man, humanly speaking. However, Jesus defeated the power of sin and of death. He is truly a warrior who fights for you.

Jesus is the greatest human warrior in all history. He is the greatest spiritual warrior of all eternity!

Napoleon Bonaparte, a great human warrior, is quoted in the book 'Jesus <u>Among</u> <u>Other Gods</u>' written by Ravi Zacharias.

Napoleon Bonaparte stated when speaking to Count Monthalon:

"Alexander, Cesar, Charlemagne, and I myself have founded great empires, but upon what did these creations of our genius depend? Upon force. Jesus alone founded His empire upon love and to this very day millions will die for Him... I think I understand something of human nature; and I tell you, all these were men, and I am a man: no one else is like Him. Jesus Christ was more than a man...I have inspired multitudes with such an enthusiastic devotion that they would have died for me...but to do this it was necessary that I should be visibly present with the electric influence of my looks, my words, of my voice. When I saw men and spoke to them, I lighted up the flames of self-devotion in their hearts...Christ alone has succeeded in so raising the mind of man toward the unseen, that it became insensible to the barriers of time and space. Across a chasm of eighteen hundred years, Jesus Christ makes a demand which is beyond all others difficult to satisfy; He asks for that which a philosopher may often seek in vain at the hands of his friends or a father of his children or a bride of her spouse, or a man of his brother. He asks for the human heart; He will have it entirely to Himself. He demands it unconditionally; and forthwith His demand is granted. Wonderful! In defiance of time and space, the soul of man, with all its powers and faculties, become an annexation to the empire of Christ. All who sincerely believe in Him, experience that remarkable, supernatural love toward Him. The phenomenon is unaccountable; it is all together beyond the scope of man's creative powers. Time, the great destroyer, is powerless to extinguish this sacred flame; time can neither exhaust its strength nor put a

limit to its range. This is it, which strikes me most; I have often thought of it. That it is which proves to me quite convincingly the Divinity of Jesus Christ". (Page 149,150).

For me it is the natural love of God. God is not supernatural, but his word clearly states, his ways are not our ways, and his thoughts are not our thoughts. The foolishness of God is far above anything anyone could ever think or imagine!

What Napoleon saw in Jesus is a power that is uncontrollable. It is the power of love. More importantly, it is the power of God's love. Napoleon is known, but he is not loved by those who did not know him. Jesus has made it possible to know God in a new and powerful way. Jesus is God's new covenant. This covenant completely replaces the old covenant.

In Jesus we can see the fulfillment of God's law. This is a law based on love and freedom of choice. Jesus does not force you to believe in him. He does not force you to receive him. Jesus is proposing to you an eternal union with God. It is a proposal. Maureen did not have to say yes when I asked her to marry me. It was her choice. For us to have a godly union, it must be based on freedom to choose. In my proposal, I was choosing her. In her acceptance of my proposal, she was choosing me.

There you have it. The most amazing thing in human existence is that God wants you to choose him. There is no demand. How could it be otherwise? Our Father in heaven is asking you to choose him. He has made the proposal and he patiently waits for you to say yes, I will be your eternal partner.

DIVINE INTERVENTION

The circumstances in my life kept me busy. I was dating. I was mother and father to an eighteen-month-old. I was in the longest real estate slump in my forty-three-year career. I was juggling loans, real estate rental, ministry, child rearing and now I was dating. Maureen was a huge motivation for me. She did not understand my life. Neither did I understand hers. However, we accepted each other and where our journeys in life had brought us.

Being a twosome brought me and Sean very close together. I had never been in a situation where I just had one person in my home. My first marriage was to a woman and her three children. Being the oldest of eight children, this was pretty easy to accept. I believe that God had in mind for me and Sean to learn about God. I did not know it then, but God was teaching me about love. His love!

Sean would follow me around the house. When I brushed my teeth, he wanted to brush his. When I shook a trash bag to open it up, Sean picked up on that. One day he got hold of a bag and began to shake it wildly. I thought, "What is he doing?" Then I realized that he was doing what I did.

I must be nuts. Just about everything reminds me of Jesus. So often Jesus said, "I do what I see the Father doing." He said the words that I have spoken are not my own. God said in Mark 9:7 *"This is my Son, whom I love. Listen to him!"* What this tells me is that Jesus is a loyal representative of God the Father.

For a time, I was Sean's focus. Yes, I was a father and mother and the G-dad. So, Sean was showing me what my Father in heaven wanted from me. My Father in heaven wants me to follow his ways, do the things he does, and be like him. Jesus is the perfect man to follow to learn the ways of God. Pay attention and a small child can teach you about yourself.

SIXTEEN

HABITS & POTTY TRAINING

otty training for Sean was well underway. He was coming along
fast. One day Sean needed to go potty, so I took him and sat him on
the toilet. I went back to what I was doing. In a fairly short-time I
heard the words "I am done"! I guess I did not respond fast enough. Again,
I heard the words "I am done." Anyone who has raised a child knows what
these words mean. I doubt that Sean's words had any relationship to the
words of Jesus when he said, "*Without me you can do nothing*" or "*Unless
you abide in me, you can do nothing.*"

However, just as this small child knew that he needed help in the
cleaning and wiping department, we all must have help from the Spirit of
Christ, if we are to be an advocate for eternal, spiritual things. It just stands
to reason those temporal beings need help doing eternal spiritual things.

Sean needed help doing an elementary human task. He needed help
from his G-dad. I do not make myself to be anything special. It is just that
from Sean's point of view I was special. From Sean's point of view, I can do
all things. I know better! However, Sean is beginning to do what he sees
me doing. In this respect, Jesus says that he does what he sees the Father
doing. God is the Father of all humanity. This makes God my Father and
your Father and Sean's Father. When he blew his breath into the lungs of
Adam, He was putting his breath into our lungs as well.

Now just as I am the example of a grown man to Sean, Jesus is your
example and my example of the personality and ways of God.

It went right over the heads of the religious leaders when Jesus with emphasis "very truly" speaks to them with a spiritual language. Jesus speaks to them in the language of eternal life. He spoke to them as a spiritual being that is forever. He spoke to them about a life that extends beyond their temporary body. Although they were the spiritual leaders, they were stuck in human comprehension and the law of Moses. Until one has a spiritual encounter or revelation with Jesus, we are stuck with our human experience.

You and I, are completely like these religious leaders who could not understand or yield to the eternal realities of what God desired to say, show and share with them at that time and with all humanity to the end of the Ages and forevermore.

Those who believe in Jesus and have been born of God will begin to see with the eyes of the Spirit. Jesus adds emphasis to the words that he had spoken in John 6:51 *"This is my flesh"*. After an argument ensued among the Jews about Jesus giving them his flesh to eat (Jn. 6:52).

Jesus spoke with an adverb and an adjective to emphasize his words. He said: *"Very truly, I tell you, unless you eat the flesh of the Son of Man and drink His blood you have no life in you"* (Jn. 6:53 NIV).

Jesus, came down in human form, walking and displaying covenantal union to the Father, who is Spirit. This is and always has been an eternal connection. Jesus' connection is spiritual. Jesus says that he only says what the Father says. He also says that he only does what he sees the Father doing.

When Jesus says to the Jews *"Unless you eat the flesh of the Son of Man and drink his blood, you have no life in you"* (Jn. 6:53 NIV), he is speaking in the eternal language of God. Jesus is speaking about you and me receiving his atonement for sin and death and his Spirit of love and mercy. This Spirit is the Spirit of God. In the eating, we are eating the everlasting bread from heaven. This is a receiving of God into your life. This is the beginning of you and I becoming a dwelling place for God. By welcoming and allowing God to live in you, you become an eternal dwelling place. Death and hell have no claim and no power over the place where God lives.

Jesus went further when He said that you must drink his blood. We all know that humanly speaking this is an offensive statement. However, again

Jesus is speaking in a spiritual reality. The blood represents a continual flow of life which the body needs. Just as the human body must have a constant flow of oxygen-filled blood, the spiritual body must have a constant flow of the Spirit.

When you are eating the body of Jesus, you are feeding on his life and his words. It is the spiritual feeding on Jesus that brings his life into yours. That is, Jesus begins to live in you. When you drink his blood, you are drinking in the wind of the Spirit. It is with your permission that this Spirit will guide your life. The Spirit will become your advocate for warning you of spiritual forces of evil that seem to constantly bombard your life. With the aid of the Spirit, you are empowered to evaluate your life and circumstances based on the life and words of Jesus on whom you are constantly feeding. The Spirit will help us to constantly examine our life and our journey with Jesus.

When Sean said, "I am done," I knew that he wanted me to do the job which was to clean his behind. Why would he want or need me to clean him? Jesus says unless you become as a little child you cannot enter into the Kingdom of Heaven. There was a reason Sean needed me to wipe his butt. He could not do the job right, so he called on someone who had the experience to do it. Jesus also told Peter that unless he (Peter) allowed Jesus to wash him, he could have no place in the ministry of Jesus, "The Christ".

To live a Christ life, we need someone who has the experience to lead us so that we can do the job right. That is why it is so important to go, not just part way, but all of the way with Jesus.

The passion of God for all humanity must be the passion of those who follow Jesus. The passion of Jesus must become your passion. I say again, the passion of Jesus must become your passion! For this to be so, you must go all the way with Jesus. He must live in you. You must rule your life from his mercy seat. Jesus will not beat you down. He will take your eternal spirit into himself. He will elevate your life from a temporal to an eternal being with a godlike character.

When Jesus takes you by the hand and leads you through his crucifixion, you will pass through the tunnel of death with Jesus. When you go all the way with Jesus, his words will begin to speak to you in the eternal language of God. Then you will receive those words with understanding and delight. The words of Jesus when speaking with Martha at Lazarus' tomb will become your words of life. Listen: "*Whoever lives by believing in me will never die*" (Jn. 11:26 in part NIV).

Sean is watching me. He is serious about being like me and doing the things that I do. Before we finish this cleaning and wiping job, I must tell you that I have developed over the years some of what you might say different hygiene principles. Believe me, Sean has been watching.

Sitting on the potty Sean will speak words that will quickly travel to my ears in the kitchen. He says, "I am done", I know this means it is time for me to finish the job. I go into the bathroom, take off about two squares of toilet paper (the squares are thick). I fold the two squares together. Then I make the first pass. I fold the squares again for the second pass to see whether or not I get additional tissue. Some clean ups are tougher than others. I start to flush the toilet, but Sean protests. He wants to do the flushing. I let him. I think that we are done.

However, Sean still with a naked bottom takes hold of a short stepladder which we keep close at hand for retrieving things above the stacked washer dryer and our high shelves. Sean pulls the ladder which is unfolded and locked in place over to the sink. I am thinking. What is he up to? He gets the ladder where he wants it. Then he begins to climb. He gets high enough so that his butt is just above the sink. At this time, he surprises me as he turns on the water. Then he turns and leans his butt over the sink. I can still visualize his movement as he leans forward on the ladder. Then, as if in slow motion, he rotates his backside over the sink. Here we have a bare-bottom boy with his bottom over the edge of the sink. It suddenly dawns on me that Sean has seen this feat done by someone. He is just doing...I do not know whether I hate to admit this or not.

Please do not think that I am sacrilegious with the following words of Jesus; "*Very truly, the Son can do nothing by himself; He can do only what he sees the Father doing, because whatever the Father does the Son also does*". Jesus says in John 10:34 concerning scripture; "*Is it not written in your law, I have said you are gods*" (Jn. 10:34 in part NIV – see also Ps. 82:1, 6).

I have said the above to emphasize the importance of words and habits when we are in fact gods or lords over young children. We are seen and we are being watched by the innocent. Good or bad young children pick up on our words and our actions.

Where did Sean pick up on this hanging your butt over the sink after a number two experience? There is no doubt where he learned it. You know this was a personal and intimate thing between me and Sean until one day I was caught by my wife. I moved so quickly that I almost hurt myself. Well, Sean was waiting, and I knew what he expected. I finished the clean- up job.

Even now I can see the scene in the bathroom over and over. It was time spent and the love given and received that built a special bond between me and Sean. It was intimate times. It was neck rides or horsey, go-to-town and don't-fall-down. It was a little boy coming down the stairs dragging his blanket seeking closeness. It is a belly laugh where the child seems to lead in the laughter.

Sean and the boys have taught me about how my God wants a closeness and a personal intimate one-on-one relationship. The joy that I have in my boys is the joy we offer to our Father in heaven when we include Him in our laughter, our joy and all of the parts of our life. I now know without any doubt that God desires closeness with me just as I rejoice in my closeness and my relationship with my boys.

There should never be any resentment or envy because of this beautiful relationship. This is a gift from God that teaches me about greater love, deeper love, more passionate love, and or enduring love that will never end. It makes me want to be like that song "I am just a love machine". However, I want to be the love of God's love machine. That kind of love will always be good. That kind of love brings with it a power that is stronger than death. It is eternal and the love of God will not return void.

With his ability to love his enemies, Jesus defeated the power of evil. Jesus defeated the power of death. Satan, the ruler of this world, now stands condemned.

Our Father in heaven is this day proposing to you. He is offering you the hand of his Son in marriage. You are invited to the wedding feast. You are invited into God's eternal realm. You are invited to be a part of the empire of Christ. Jesus is offering you his life to live. The proposal is on the table. God's banquet has been prepared for his children. Pull a chair up. Sit down and eat the eternal food from Heaven. Stay tuned!

EPILOGUE

It's been a while since I wrote the words in this book, but God is still teaching me. I have seen enough heartache in life. I have seen enough death. I know about war and conflict. I know about a desperate humanity seeking life in all the wrong places. I know about the hurt and pain in families. I know older people who recognize that this temporal life is passing away. I know about doubt and faith. And, I have experienced a complete lack of faith. I now know that Jesus saw the plight of humanity. I know about his tears, and now he is satisfied that I truly want to know him. He knows that my prayers are sincere.

One day doing dishes, I was talking with my Father and I said "Father, help me to know Jesus more personally." I was rinsing a bowl. Drying the bowl, I turned toward the cabinet to put the bowl away. Before I got to the cabinet I prayed "Father, have mercy on me". This was a Spirit aided prayer. The Spirit expressed to me that God had long ago placed this prayer in my heart and soul. The soil of my heart and soul had been prepared to receive the eternal teaching of God.

I prayed for mercy because I knew that to truly know Jesus was to be willing to suffer with him. I had weighed the cost, and in my heart, I knew that the joy of knowing Jesus would greatly surpass the pain of dying with him. To die with him, I give up the destruction of the mind and heart when I harbor unforgiveness. I say no to hate, lies and deceit. I have learned to love my enemies and even pray for them.

He endured the cross because of the joy set before him. Isaiah said about twenty-seven hundred years ago that after he has suffered, he will see the light of life and be satisfied (Is. 11:53a). Jesus lives in the power and Spirit of God.

Paul says that the followers of Jesus have available to them the mind of Christ. To have this mind is to mourn for a lost world.

What will satisfy Jesus? Isaiah writes "the light of life". This is a light like no other. It is the light that darkness cannot overcome. It is the light which death cannot extinguish. Jesus sees this light carried by the eternal Spirit which he promised to send to all those who follow him.

There is a scripture which says that only those the Father draws to Jesus can hear him. The apostle Paul writes that it is better to be known by God than to know God. You could ask why is God not drawing all people? That is a valid question. The Spirit tells me that the Father will only draw those who have reached a point in their lives concerning God that they have become willing to give up all traditions and doctrines, and teachings of man in order that they may truly know the truth that comes from the heart of God. Everyone has their truth, but human truths are subjective based on personal experiences. The truth Jesus spoke about is eternal truth that are the heart and life of the Father flowing to and through us so we can all live in constant reciprocation of what the Father originally intended in the Garden of Eden before sin defiled it.

Infants and very young children are very vulnerable. They are also very innocent before the world around them begins to destroy their innocence. They place their heart in your hands and you know that their heart is true. You know that they love you without prejudice.

When you or I come to a place in our life, consciously or unconsciously, where above all else we want truth, this is when our Father will introduce us to Jesus. You see, our Father is the Spirit that deals in truth. When the apostle Paul says that it is better to be known by God than to know God (Gal. 4:9), he is saying that *"Whoever loves God is known by God."* (1 Co. 9:3 NIV).

To love God is not a conscious effort. Like the boys loving me or me loving the boys is not a conscious effort. It is the unseen substance that flows from heart to heart. When it is the God- Kind of love, it takes on a new eternal dimension. Spiritually speaking you have entered into the eternal realm of God. In this dimension and in this realm, you have the power of love which is more powerful than death. It is the unconscious desire within your heart for truth. When you have been fed a lie even though it may have been unintentional, or it may have come from someone who loves you, it is still a lie.

For a lot of us it is when the world is whipping us or breaking us that we come to the place in our life where we are seeking understanding. Our heart cries out to be understood. To be loved without question. However, those around us are so wrapped up in their search of a greater human life that they are blinded from true life. You are sinking, but no one throws you a life jacket. The spiritual forces of evil and destruction are all around disguised as life. In reality they are evil, darkness and death.

God is watching. He is not watching to condemn you. He is patiently waiting for your heart to come into alignment with a heart that he knows. He does not know the heart of evil, of judgment or the heart of destruction.

You see, God is good. He is good all the time. When God sees your heart that is breaking and crying out for truth, mercy and love, He is like the father who ran to meet his wayward son. When life has whipped you and your heart is seeking truth and love and when that heart within you has repented before you have ever said a word, God will put his arms around you and welcome you into Himself. God knows this heart of repentance and knows that this heart is prepared to receive his love.

This is when the Father draws you to Jesus. Why now? Until you truly seek the truth of God without bias, you will be like the Pharisees, the Jews, and the teachers of the law, and others who rejected Jesus. They rejected him and they still reject him today when their religion, traditions and doctrines override God's truth. There is no way that I could be taught by children without the aid of the Holy Spirit.

I see the hand of God at work from the time I prayed for companionship. My human prayer was not exactly in line with the prayer of the Spirit of truth. As a matter of fact, they were not in line at all. However, since I am known by God, the Spirit of God understands the deep needs within my heart.

If you are still with me, we have journeyed along with the Spirit. My journey with my boys continues on. My Father who created me in his image is continuing his work. I am so glad that the Father knows me and that I continue to be taught by the Spirit of truth.

I want my boys and my family and my friends to be known by God and taught by the Spirit of Truth. I want them to know this Spirit of eternal life. I want them to know within their heart that God knows them and loves them with a love that overpowers death.

There is no greater feeling than to know without a doubt that you are God's eternal child who is born, not of human means, but who is born of God.

Jesus wanted to leave his followers with peace, comfort and joy as he prepared to return to the Father.

Jesus has shown us the way to go back to Eden, the garden of pleasure and delight, a place of eternal peace, comfort and joy that we are created to have with our Father who is in heaven. Our destiny is to become like Jesus. Our destiny is to have an eternal body. Jesus left his followers with the promise, that an advocate would come to us so that we might begin to experience the eternal reality of what God has in store for those who love Him. I want my children and my family to be able to celebrate my departure with peace and joy as they learn to live the reality of God's eternity.

I see waters, mountains, and beautiful streams and waterfalls. I see green forest and meadows. I see the river of the water of life flowing abundantly. I see the trees on each side of the river bearing the beautiful fruit of healing. I see Jesus walking towards me. He has a broad smile and bright eyes like Jacques. He is beautiful. I hear the sound of music. It is in perfect harmony.

I have entered the paradise of God. I see a bear and calf together. They are being led by a young child. It is like a fantasyland, but it is not a fantasy. It is God's reality. This is my destination. Do not mourn! Celebrate with food and dancing and music. My God is above all gods, friends and family. My prayer is that you fall in love with the eternal man. He will take you to God's paradise. Amen

PHOTO GALLERY

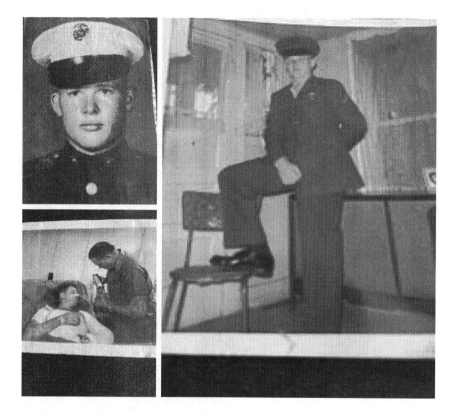

Dwight as a young Marine, before and after injuries

Left above -Jacques and Jaden   **Sean**

G-Dad competing in Senior Games

Sean and his sister

Jacques

Jaden

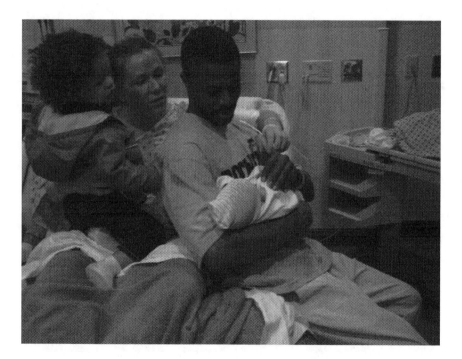

From Left – Jacques, Julia, Reico, Jaden
(Birth of Jaden)

G-Dad and Jaden

3 Amigos & Sidekick- From Left – Aaron, Jacques, Sean and Jaden

From Left – Jacques and Jaden

Jacques

Julia and Jacques

Julia and Jacques

Jacques and Jaden

Sean the Woodcutter

Printed in the United States
by Baker & Taylor Publisher Services